Level 2–3

EARTH SCIENCE
ACTIVITIES
for the Elementary Classroom
(KSAM)

Ernest L. Kern, Senior Editor

David Munn, Project Manager
Dale Lyle, Editor
Lisa Gollihue, Designer and Illustrator
Ruth Linstromberg, Illustrator
Yvonne Cronin, Typesetter
Carol L. Leung, Computer Specialist

CURRICULUM ASSOCIATES®, Inc.
North Billerica, MA 01862

ISBN 1-55915-957-X
©1997—Curriculum Associates, Inc.
North Billerica, MA 01862

PREFACE

Earth Science Activities for the Elementary Classroom: Level 2–3 is an outgrowth of the KSAM (**K**–6 **S**cience **A**nd **M**ath) Program, a highly successful elementary-teacher inservice program in science and mathematics that has served over 15,000 teachers since its inception in 1985 at Southeast Missouri State University. In an effort to further meet the needs of elementary teachers beyond those addressed in inservice training, KSAM conducted summer writing conferences in which educators from all levels participated, the largest group, by far, being K–6 classroom teachers. The larger number of elementary teachers was appropriate based on our belief in the old saying that the best solutions are produced by those most experienced in the problem. The charge to these educators was to develop quality, practical, affectively palatable, content-sound, process-based student activities in K–6 science and mathematics that worked well both for the teacher and the student. The result was the publication of the KSAM Earth Science Series, as well as the KSAM Physical Science Series, KSAM Biological Science Series, and KSAM Mathematics Series. Thus, the activities in all the series guides were developed *by* K–6 teachers *for* K–6 teachers. This is as it should be. For who better understands the problems and needs of the classroom teacher? Who better understands elementary students and how they think, how they learn, and how they react? Who is in a better position to develop a publication that will be of maximum value to elementary teachers and their students? The answer is obviously the teachers who directly experience those classroom situations each day.

The success of those educators in meeting their charge is represented by the many thousands of teachers who have successfully used the KSAM guides on a regional level prior to national publication. In fact, development of these materials within a major teacher inservice program has allowed for the repeated classroom testing and refinement of activities, resulting in a set of experiences for students that do, indeed, work well. Both success and quality are also indicated by the awards received by the KSAM Program and its science and math activity guide series, including a Meritorious Program Award (1989, U.S. Department of Education) and the Christa McAuliffe Showcase for Excellence Award (1994, American Association of State Colleges and Universities). The KSAM Program was also selected for inclusion in Promising Practices in Mathematics and Science (1994, U.S. Department of Education). Most of all, the success of these materials is mirrored in the faces of the many students who have discovered science and math to be an exciting adventure of discovery.

Earth Science Activities for the Elementary Classroom: Level 2–3 is dedicated to all elementary teachers, for without question, they are the most important element and influence in a person's total education.

Ernest L. Kern
Senior Editor

ACKNOWLEDGMENTS

It would take several pages to list, by name, all the individuals who have been involved in the development of this activity guide. Rather, let it suffice to say that deep appreciation is extended to all the elementary, secondary, and university educators who participated on the writing teams during the initial development of activities. Gratitude is also expressed to the many school districts and K–6 teachers that participated in the classroom testing of activities. Appreciation is also extended to Southeast Missouri State University, the National Science Foundation, and the Southwestern Bell Foundation, who partially supported the writing of this guide through grant funding. Finally, Nancy Pfeiffer, Staci Beussink, and Carrie Johnson deserve special mention for their dedication, loyalty, and hard work in seeing this project through.

TABLE OF CONTENTS

INTRODUCTION

Purpose

The primary purpose of the series *Earth Science Activities for the Elementary Classroom: (Level K–1, Level 2–3, and Level 4–6)* is to provide elementary teachers with appropriate, quality materials for the enhancement of both science instruction and science learning in their classrooms; to aid them in their efforts to demonstrate to students not only the absolute necessity of a science competency in today's society, but also the simple fact that science can be fun and exciting. Because research has so clearly shown the strong relationship between the cognitive and affective domains—that students, at all levels, learn best those things that they enjoy or find interesting or feel are important—this guide stresses the incorporation of the science processes in hands-on activities that not only feature content integrity but also elicit positive affective responses from students.

Science is a required subject in the elementary curricula in most districts; yet, unfortunately, by the time students reach the middle school or junior high level, far too many have become disenchanted with science. In short, they just don't like it. It appears that much of the explanation for their "turnoff" can be attributed to two factors.

The first factor is the way in which science is presented or portrayed to the students. Science is as much a verb as a noun; one does science as well as learns about science. Science is an activity just as much as it is a body of knowledge. In fact, that body of knowledge—the content of science—developed (and continually expands) as a result of the doing of science. The science processes (see Appendix) represent a framework of actions or operations that constitute the activity of science and the obtainment of content. Make no mistake, the content of science is vitally important. Content represents previous understandings that allow new scientific endeavors to begin at a point beyond the point at which previous endeavors ended. Content contains the terminology or language of science that allows more effective communication among scientists. And it is content that fuels applied science and technology—those efforts that provide society the myriad advancements that make life easier and better. Thus, science is a blend of both process and content. Historically, however, it has not been so portrayed and presented in many elementary, secondary, and college classrooms. Instead, it has been the content of science that has been stressed, sometimes to the complete disregard of the process of science. Consequently, students come away with a distorted perception of science. They see it only as facts, figures, terms, principles, and theories that must be memorized. No wonder many students find it boring! The content provided to students needs to be balanced with ample opportunities to engage also in the "doing of science"—to manipulate, to observe, to experiment, to discover. Students need to experience the whole of science to perceive it as the exciting adventure it really is.

The second factor contributing to student turnoff is that many concepts in science are inherently abstract; yet, most students at the K–6 level are in the concrete stage of mental development and thus experience difficulty thinking (learning) in abstractions. Along these same lines, it should be noted that the lecture, undoubtedly the most commonly used approach for the teaching of science, is an extremely abstract mode of instruction.

The activities in this guide are designed to provide students with concrete-level experiences to represent and/or supplement science concepts. In essence, they provide a "bridge" for the concrete thinker to better understand those concepts. In addition to promoting mastery of content material, the activities also promote the development of the science processes, including critical thinking and reasoning, and at the same time foster interest, creativity, and enthusiasm. In short, students will find these activities to be enjoyable and exciting avenues leading to a better understanding and appreciation of the world around them.

Earth Science Activities for the Elementary Classroom: Level 2–3 is not intended as a 2–3 science curriculum even though most Earth Science topics covered at this level are addressed by the activities. Rather, this guide is specifically designed to supplement and enrich any existing curriculum.

Activity Format

The activities in this guide were written for teachers. All activities follow a standard format developed by teachers to be of maximum utilitarian value. In fact, teachers will find the activities to be much like lesson plans. The format consists of ten components.

1. **Primary Content:** identifies the major content thrust(s) of the activity.

2. **Process Skills:** lists those science processes used by students in completing the activity. A complete listing of the processes, including definitions, is included in the Appendix. The processes listed under this heading will follow the same order as that presented in the appendix which, generally, runs from less complex to more complex.

3. **Prior Student Knowledge:** identifies any special knowledge, skills, or understandings needed by students to effectively complete the activity. When none are listed, normal skills and abilities for the general grade level of the activity are assumed.

4. **Group Size:** indicates the recommended size of student groups for effective learning. Entries under this heading typically fall into one of three categories: individual, groupings of various sizes, or whole class. Of course, availability of materials, class size, and teacher objectives may necessitate adjustments of the group size.

5. **Pre-Activity Preparation:** lists and describes any special materials and/or preparatory work that the teacher needs to do prior to doing the actual activity. The obtainment of typical or common materials is not included here; however, such materials are identified under the Materials Per Group heading.

6. **Materials Per Group:** a detailed listing of all materials, supplies, and equipment needed by each student group (as indicated under Group Size) for the activity. This approach makes calculating materials needed for a given activity much simpler. Whenever a listed item is intended for other than the group size previously identified in the activity, such will be indicated with that item listing. With very few exceptions, only easy-to-obtain materials are called for, usually items found in most classrooms or homes. It is assumed that every student will have pencils and paper available, therefore, those items are not included in the materials listing.

7. **Teacher Information:** content information that may be needed by the teacher to fully understand the activity concept(s) and/or to effectively direct the activity in the classroom. It should be noted that this information is intended for the teacher; there is no implication that this material be wholly transferred to students. How much, if any, of the information contained in this section is presented to students is solely a decision of the teacher based upon grade level, objectives, and student abilities.

8. **Procedure:** a detailed, easy-to-follow listing of the steps necessary to set up and complete the activity. Also included for most activities are a whole-class introduction and a post-activity closure, both often in the form of suggested questioning sequences and/or discussion topics which the teacher can adapt to the appropriate student level.

9. **Extensions and Adaptations:** identifies appropriate activity extensions and adaptations to aid in the further development or reinforcement of the activity concepts.

10. **Reproducibles and Supplements:** while not listed as an individual heading, all reproducibles that accompany the activity are identified in the Pre-Activity Preparation section and the Materials Per Group section, as well as in the Procedure. Reproducibles that have specific answers are included in the Answer Key. Supplements include pages with instructions for the teacher to make items required for certain activities. Usually these pages do not need to be reproduced.

Post-Activity Closure

Educational research has long supported the fact that post-activity closure is extremely important to concept attainment. Such closure may take many forms: an informal class discussion, a specific questioning sequence, review of the activity procedure and the results or answers obtained, etc. Most of the activities in this guide contain closure to one degree or another. Frequently, when time starts running short, the "closure section" is the easiest to omit. You are encouraged to retain closure to all activities, and when possible, to expand on the suggestions presented in this guide. When time does start running short, remember that closure can always be carried over to a subsequent day.

Activity Location

In some guides, finding the right activity to supplement a given topic is quite a chore and often necessitates reviewing a number of different activities before the right one is located. *Earth Science Activities for the Elementary Classroom* incorporates several aids to help facilitate this task.

The Table of Contents groups the activities by major topics. Abbreviated Activity Descriptions follow the Introduction. These descriptions stress the content nature of the activities—usually the first concern of a teacher. The activity numbers and page numbers are also included for quick reference.

National Science Content Standards

The National Research Council in cooperation with a number of other scientific and education associations, has established a set of national science content standards for all grade levels, K–12, in an effort to improve the quality of school science. The standards are divided into three categories based upon grade level: K–4, 5–8, and 9–12.

All the activities in *Earth Science for the Elementary Classroom: Level 2–3* have been correlated to science content standards for grades K–4. That correlation, and a listing of the standards, can be found in Appendix B, pages 160–163.

A Note on Safety

There is a need to be concerned about student safety in any hands-on activity in any subject. Of course, the degree of risk varies depending on the materials involved, the age and maturity level of the students, and the degree of adult supervision. Teachers sometimes think that they need be concerned only with those activities that involve heat, volatile chemicals or materials, or potentially toxic substances. However, even seemingly harmless items can become a safety threat in the more open and unstructured environment that typically accompanies hands-on learning.

In utilizing the activities in this guide, students should be closely supervised at all times. In addition, you are urged to exercise caution and good judgment in all matters that might affect the safety of students. It is also recommended that if a student feels uncomfortable or sensitive about participating in a given activity, an alternate experience should be provided for that student.

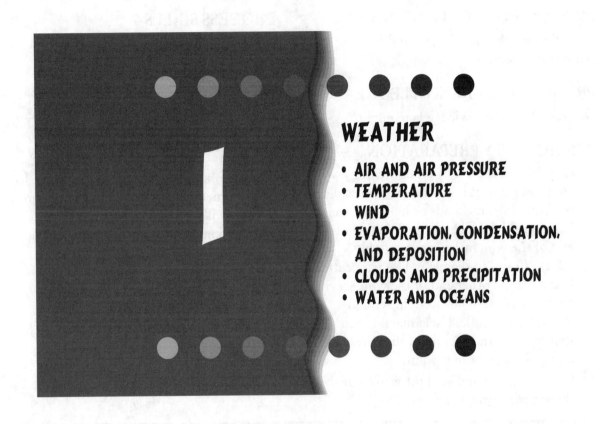

WEATHER

- AIR AND AIR PRESSURE
- TEMPERATURE
- WIND
- EVAPORATION, CONDENSATION, AND DEPOSITION
- CLOUDS AND PRECIPITATION
- WATER AND OCEANS

BALLOON KEBAB

PRIMARY CONTENT

Attention grabber for the Air and
Air Pressure section

PRIOR STUDENT KNOWLEDGE

No special prior knowledge is required.

PRE-ACTIVITY PREPARATION

1. Construct a skewer by straightening a wire
   coat hanger. Get it as straight as possible
   by flattening any bends or kinks with a
   hammer. Make a handle by bending one
   end of the wire into a circle roughly
   7.5 cm (3 in.) in diameter. Use wire cutters
   to cut off the other end of the wire, leaving
   about 61 cm (2 ft) of straight section
   beyond the handle. Use a metal file to
   sharpen the straight end of the wire into
   a very sharp, tapering point.
2. Coat the point and straight section of the
   skewer with petroleum jelly.

PROCESS SKILLS

Observing, inferring

GROUP SIZE

Whole class

MATERIALS PER GROUP

- 1 skewer (for teacher demonstration)
- 1 large balloon, 20 cm–41 cm (8 in.–16 in.)
  in diameter, (for teacher demonstration)
  (You will probably need more than
  1 balloon since demands for repeat
  performances are likely.)

TEACHER INFORMATION

The reason that most balloons pop when pierced has
to do with air pressure. The air pressure in an inflated
balloon is higher than the air pressure outside the
balloon. Air always attempts to move from an area
of high pressure toward an area of lower pressure.
When balloon material is pierced, air tries to rush
from inside the balloon to outside through the small
hole made by the piercing (much like air leaving an
inflated balloon when its nozzle is opened). The thin
balloon-wall material cannot withstand this onrush
of air. The material thus blows out (tears) with an
accompanying rapid escape of air, making a loud
pop in the process.

Because of the way in which balloons are made, balloon
material is thicker at and immediately adjacent to the
nozzle and at the end opposite the nozzle. Because it is
thicker and stronger, the material at these two spots
can (usually) withstand the onrush of air toward and
through the hole made by the skewer (in this activity)
or any pointed object without bursting. Thus, no pop
or explosion!

Petroleum jelly is used as a lubricant to keep the
skewer from tearing the balloon material during the
skewering process; it is not meant to be a sealant.
It is recommended that you use new balloons for
skewering because rubber weakens with age. It is also
suggested that you practice Procedure steps 6–9 a few
times before you do the activity in the classroom.

PROCEDURE

1. Introduce the activity by asking students what happens to an inflated balloon when it is stuck with a sharp object. *(It pops, of course.)* Inform them that it is an aspect of air called air pressure that is responsible for the popping of a balloon.

2. (Optional) If consistent with your objectives and the content background of the students, ask the class if they have any idea why a balloon pops when pierced (see Teacher Information).

3. Tell the class that just in case some students have never seen a balloon pop, you are going to pierce a balloon using a sharp wire. Show class the skewer.

4. Now display a deflated balloon. Let a couple of students examine it to confirm to the rest of the class that it is just a normal balloon.

5. Inflate the balloon and tie it off. For best results, only inflate it about three-fourths full, not to total capacity. Again ask the class what is going to happen when you stick the sharp wire into the balloon. *(Students will all agree that the balloon is going to pop!)*

6. Hold the inflated balloon firmly between one arm and your body (as if you had it in a head lock), the end opposite the balloon's nozzle facing your free arm. Holding the skewer by its handle with your free hand, *gently* place the point on the extra-thick rubber spot at the end opposite the nozzle of the balloon. You can easily identify the exact spot: it will be darker than the rest of the balloon material (when inflated) and/or there will be a tiny nipple.

7. Gently apply inward pressure on the skewer while, at the same time, giving the skewer a back-and-forth turning motion by rotating your wrist. The skewer will soon pierce the balloon, with no associated pop!

8. Now carefully push the skewer through the inside of the balloon, making sure you don't touch the inside walls with the point, until the point is positioned immediately adjacent to the nozzle. With the same motion as in step 7, push the skewer through.

9. The balloon is now completely kebabbed on the skewer. It is really fun to see! You may even spin the balloon around the skewer if you wish and/or add another balloon.

10. Students will be in a state of awe! With this activity, you've grabbed their attention and created interest for the section on air and air pressure.

11. Pull the skewer out and quickly pop the balloon by sticking it with the skewer in a less-thick rubber area. This really amazes those students who thought you were using a trick balloon.

12. You may decide to explain this trick or not. The latter proves to be a lot of fun—not knowing how you did it will really capture students' interest!

EXTENSIONS AND ADAPTATIONS

1. Use small, round balloons and skewer through 3 or 4 at one time. Note, however, that small balloons have a tendency to pop a little easier than large balloons.

2. Leave a balloon on the skewer and time how long it takes for it to completely deflate. They've been known to stay inflated for up to an entire day.

3. Try the activity using other sharp objects to pierce the balloon—a sewing needle or a compass point, for example.

4. Because of the sharp point on the skewer, it is not recommended that you allow students at the 2–3 level to attempt the balloon kebab. However, should you decide to let them try, be certain that you supervise closely.

5. The other activities comprising the Air and Air Pressure section in this guide are all appropriate extensions.

SILVER SPIRAL

PRIMARY CONTENT
- Understanding the relationship between air temperature and air density
- Understanding that warm air rises

PRIOR STUDENT KNOWLEDGE
The concept of the molecular makeup of air

PRE-ACTIVITY PREPARATION
Construct and position a silver spiral as directed in the supplement Making and Positioning a Silver Spiral (page 6).

PROCESS SKILLS
Observing, inferring, hypothesizing

GROUP SIZE
Whole class

MATERIALS PER GROUP
- 1 positioned silver spiral
- 1 hot plate (for teacher use)
- 1 student desk
- 1 extension cord (if needed) (for teacher use)

TEACHER INFORMATION

As air is heated, the motion of the molecules comprising the air is increased. This, in turn, results in greater molecular spacing—the air expands. Consequently, there are fewer molecules per given volume of air than was the case prior to the heating. Fewer molecules means that the volume of air has less mass or weight, or in other words, a decreased density. (Density equals mass per volume.) Being less dense and lighter than surrounding cooler air (air that did not undergo heating), warm air rises. In this activity, air is heated by a hot plate. The air expands, its density decreases (it becomes lighter), and the air rises. The upward movement of the air past the silver spiral causes the spiral to rotate. Although not addressed in this activity, when air is cooled, the reverse process occurs: molecular motion and spacing decrease, density increases, and the denser, heavier air sinks.

In our atmosphere, air movement associated with heating and cooling is very common; it is called convection. In fact, many summer thunderstorms are created by heating and the resultant air motion, as the sun heats some spots or areas of the surface more than others.

PROCEDURE

1. Begin the activity by directing students' attention to the hanging silver spiral. Ask them to describe its motion. *(The spiral should be motionless or almost so, especially if you have curtailed air motion in the room.)*

2. Ask a student to position himself/herself directly beneath the hanging spiral. Crouching or kneeling will probably be necessary.

3. With his/her head tilted back about 30 cm–45 cm (12 in.–18 in.) below the spiral, have the student blow gently (at least at first) upward toward the spiral for thirty seconds or so.

4. Have the class observe the spiral and then ask questions such as:

   • Is the spiral in motion now? If so, can you describe its motion? *(The spiral now has a turning or rotating motion.)*

   • What is causing the motion? *(air movement due to the student's blowing)*

   • In what direction is the air moving that is causing the motion? *(upward or rising)*

   • What happened to the spiral's motion after the student stopped blowing? *(It gradually ceased.)*

   • Can we conclude, then, that upward air movement is necessary for spiral motion? *(yes)*

5. If time allows, you may wish to let other students take turns blowing the spiral.

6. After all blowing has been completed and the spiral is again motionless, ask the class if there is air movement acting on the spiral. *(No, the spiral is still.)*

7. Position the desk and hot plate directly beneath the spiral. Set the hot plate on medium to high heat (or the heat setting that you observed during pre-activity experimentation to produce the best results). If the hot plate is already turned on and preheated, it will save time.

8. Again have students observe the spiral's motion. Ask questions such as:

   • Is the spiral again in motion? If so, describe its motion. *(The spiral begins to turn and rotate again, rapidly in many cases.)*

   • Does that mean that air movement is acting on the spiral? *(yes)*

   • In what direction must the air be moving? *(The air must be moving upward or rising.)*

   • Nobody is blowing air now. What, then, is causing the upward movement of air? *(It must be because the hot plate heats the air, and the warm air rises.)*

   • Is this strong evidence that warm air rises? *(yes)*

   • Do you think that if air outside were heated rapidly (say by solar energy), that air would rise? *(yes)*

9. Remove the desk and hot plate. Have students observe as the spiral's motion gradually ceases. Ask the class why the spiral's motion has stopped. *(Since air is no longer being heated, upward movement of the air stops.)*

10. Ask students if they have any ideas as to why air rises when it is heated. (See Teacher Information; explain the relationship between air density and temperature as necessary.)

11. Conclude the activity by asking students to identify other examples showing that warm air rises. (Examples include: smoke rising out of a chimney, attics being exceptionally hot in the summer, hot air balloons, heat rising over a kitchen stove or space heater, and the burst of heat felt on the face—as opposed to the lower body—when the door to a hot oven is opened.)

EXTENSIONS AND ADAPTATIONS

1. You can set up for observation several silver spirals, each with a different heat source (differing energy outputs). Examples of heat sources might include: small candle, large candle, hot plate set on low, hot plate set on high, and so on.

2. You can also make spirals from the flat portions of paper plates. Students can decorate these spirals as they desire.

3. Make simple hot air balloons using plastic grocery bags or the plastic bags available in the vegetable and fruit departments in supermarkets. Use a large candle as a heat source.

4. Related activities Full of Hot Air on page 7 and 'Round and 'Round She Goes on page 62.

SILVER SPIRAL

MAKING AND POSITIONING A SILVER SPIRAL

Materials
- 1 disposable aluminum pie pan
- Scissors
- 1 length of thread, 2.4 m (8 ft)
- 1 needle, pin, or compass point
- Masking tape
- 1 student desk
- 1 hot plate
- 1 small step ladder

Directions

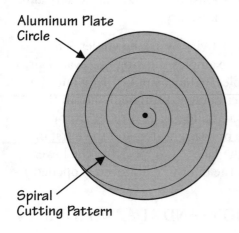

Aluminum Plate Circle

Spiral Cutting Pattern

1. Use scissors to cut away the side from a disposable aluminum pie plate, leaving a flat circle.

2. Starting from the outside of the circle, cut a continuous strip about 2.5 cm (1 in.) wide that spirals in to the center of the circle.

3. Punch a pin-size hole in the center of the spiral.

4. Tie an enlarged knot at the end of the thread. From the inside of the spiral, insert the unknotted end of the thread through the hole, pulling the thread from the outside until the knot catches on the inside.

5. On the day of the activity (but without students being present) use tape to suspend the spiral from the ceiling or light fixture. The spiral should hang to a length such that when a student's desk with a hot plate is positioned directly under the spiral, the bottom of the spiral is about 30 cm–60 cm (12 in.–24 in.) above the hot plate.

6. While the results of the Silver Spiral activity are dependable under a range of conditions, you may want to experiment with different heat settings on the hot plate and/or different distances of the spiral above the hot plate to get the best results for use in Procedure step 7.

7. For best results, you should curtail other air motions in the room as much as possible.

8. After you have attached the spiral, remove the desk and hot plate until the appropriate time during the activity.

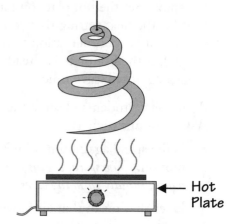

Hot Plate

FULL OF HOT AIR

PRIMARY CONTENT
- Understanding the relationship between air temperature and air density
- Understanding that warm air rises and cold air sinks

PRIOR STUDENT KNOWLEDGE
The concept of a balance scale and the concept of the molecular makeup of air

PRE-ACTIVITY PREPARATION
At the center on the outside bottom of a medium-sized paper bag (the exact size is not critical), attach a small (1.3 cm [$\frac{1}{2}$ in.]) piece of masking tape. Punch a pin-sized hole through the tape and bag at the center point of the bag's bottom. Tie an enlarged knot at the end of a 30 cm (12 in.) length of thread. From the inside of the bag, insert the unknotted end of the thread through the hole, pulling it from the outside until the knot catches on the inside. Repeat the process for a second, identical bag.

PROCESS SKILLS
Observing, comparing, inferring, hypothesizing

GROUP SIZE
Whole class

MATERIALS PER GROUP
- 2 prepared paper bags (for teacher demonstration; see Pre-Activity Preparation)
- 2 yardsticks or metersticks (for teacher demonstration)
- 1 length of string, 30 cm–60 cm (1 ft–2 ft), (for teacher demonstration)
- 2 or 3 heavy books (for teacher demonstration)
- 1 regular-sized candle (not a small birthday candle) (for teacher demonstration)
- Matches (for teacher demonstration)
- Masking tape (for teacher demonstration)
- 1 fire extinguisher (for teacher demonstration)

TEACHER INFORMATION

As air is heated, the motion of the molecules comprising the air is increased. This, in turn, results in greater molecular spacing—the air expands. Consequently, there are fewer molecules per given volume of air than was the case prior to the heating. Fewer molecules means that the volume of air has less mass or weight, or in other words, a decreased density. (Density equals mass per volume.) Being less dense and lighter than surrounding cooler air (air that did not undergo heating), warm air rises. In this activity, air is heated by a candle. It expands, its density

decreases (it becomes lighter), and the air rises. Some of that warm, rising air is caught and trapped in the paper bag, causing the bag to rise as well. When air is cooled, the reverse process occurs: molecular motion and spacing decrease, density increases, and the denser, heavier air sinks.

In our atmosphere, air movement associated with heating and cooling is very common; it is called convection. In fact, many summer thunderstorms are created by heating and the resultant air motion as the sun heats some spots or areas of the surface more than others.

PROCEDURE

1. Begin the activity by telling students to observe the smoke that is produced when you light a match. Light the match and ask students questions such as:

    - In which direction did the smoke go? *(The smoke rose.)*

    - Do you have any ideas as to why the smoke went up? (See Teacher Information; listen to responses but do not provide answers at this time.)

    - During the summer, have you ever been in the attic of a house? If so, what is the temperature there compared to the temperature on other floors of the house? *(It's much hotter in the attic.)*

    - Why do you think attics are almost always hotter than the other floors of a house? (Again, allow discussion but do not provide answers at this time.)

2. Inform the class that today's activity will help provide answers to these questions.

3. Lay a meterstick or yardstick flat on a table or desk so that one end of the stick extends about 20 cm (8 in.) over the edge. Set several books on the desk portion of the stick to stabilize it. This will be the supporting stick. (See illustration at Procedure step 6.)

4. Tie the free end of the thread extending from the bottom of one of the open bags about 2.5 cm (1 in.) from one end of a second meterstick or yardstick (the balance stick). Use enough thread so that about 5 cm–7.6 cm (2 in.–3 in.) of thread separates the bag from the stick. Repeat this with the second bag at the other end of the stick, making sure the thread length equals that of the first bag. Secure each thread tie with a small piece of masking tape.

5. Tie one end of the string around the center of the balance stick. Tie the other end of the string about 2.5 cm (1 in.) from the extended end of the supporting stick so that the bags on the balance stick are about 30.5 cm–45.7 cm (1 ft–1½ ft) above the floor. Secure the string tie around the supporting stick with a small piece of masking tape.

6. Adjust the position of the tie around the center of the balance stick until the bags are in balance (at the same level, with the balance stick being horizontal). Secure this string position with a small piece of masking tape.

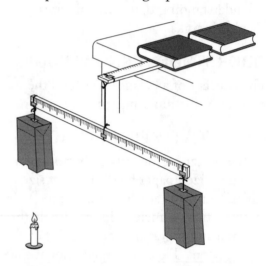

7. Tell the class that you are going to put a lighted candle under one of the bags. Ask students to guess what will happen.

8. Light the candle and hold it about 15 cm–30 cm (6 in.–12 in.) under the open end of one of the bags. Be careful not to touch the bag with the flame! Have a fire extinguisher at hand should you accidentally set the bag on fire.

9. Have students observe the results. *(The heated bag should soon begin to rise.)*

10. Remove the candle and extinguish the flame. Have students continue to observe the setup. *(As the air in the heated bag cools, that bag will sink and the balance will return to a horizontal position.)*

11. Conduct a session to discuss the results of the activity and to present explanations as needed. Include questions such as:

- Which bag rose, the heated or unheated one? *(the heated bag)*

- What was the air temperature in the bag that rose compared to the temperature in the other bag? *(The air was warmer in the bag that rose.)*

- Then what do you think made the bag rise? *(warm air)*

- Why do you think the warm air lifted the bag? (See Teacher Information; explain the relationship between air density and temperature as necessary.)

- Why did the balance stick return to a horizontal position (why did the heated bag drop) soon after I removed the candle? *(The air in the bag cooled and became denser and heavier; thus it no longer rose and lifted up on the bag.)*

- Why is it usually hotter in the attic than on the other floors of a house? *(Hot air is less dense [lighter], it rises, and then it becomes trapped in the attic.)*

- Why is it usually cooler in the basement than on the other floors of a house? *(Because cold air is denser [heavier], it sinks and then it settles in the basement.)*

- Why did the smoke from the match rise? *(The air that the smoke was in was heated by the match, so it became less dense [lighter] and it rose.)*

- Can you think of other examples showing that warm air rises? *(Examples include: hot air balloon, heat rising over a kitchen stove, and smoke rising from a fire.)*

EXTENSIONS AND ADAPTATIONS

1. Make simple hot air balloons using plastic grocery bags or the plastic bags available in the vegetable and fruit departments in supermarkets. You can use a large candle as a heat source.

2. Related activities Silver Spiral on page 4 and 'Round and 'Round She Goes on page 62.

UNWORKABLE STRAW

PRIMARY CONTENT
- Understanding that air has weight and exerts a force on other substances
- Understanding the concept of air pressure

PRIOR STUDENT KNOWLEDGE
The concept of the molecular makeup of air

PRE-ACTIVITY PREPARATION
1. Each student will need a well-cleaned plastic bottle with a screw-on cap. Smaller bottles are more convenient (soda, juice, and flavored-water bottles, for example); however, a 2 L bottle will also work. Ask students to bring these from home.
2. In each cap, punch or drill a hole just large enough to accommodate a standard-sized plastic straw. If you punch instead of drill, all the caps must be metal. To prevent the caps from bending, punch the holes from the inside out on a piece of scrap wood. If you need to enlarge the holes, use a hammer and a large-diameter nail to ream the holes. If you use a drill, either metal or plastic caps will work. Use a drill bit with a diameter slightly larger than the straw; drill the caps from the inside out on scrap wood.

3. Obtain a tube of silicone sealant or caulking (available in any hardware or home supply store).

PROCESS SKILLS
Observing, comparing, inferring, hypothesizing, identifying variables

GROUP SIZE
Individual

MATERIALS PER GROUP
- 1 plastic bottle with prepared screw-on cap (see Pre-Activity Preparation)
- 1 plastic soda straw
- Several paper towels
- 1 tube of silicone sealant or caulking (for whole class)
- Available water (for whole class)
- Masking tape (for whole class)

TEACHER INFORMATION

Because air is composed of molecules, and since molecules are actual bits of matter, air must have weight. Anything that has weight must exert a force—the greater the weight, the greater the force. If a book, for example, is placed on someone's hand, that person feels the force of the book's weight. The thicker and heavier the book, the greater the force that is felt. Because air has weight, it, too, exerts a force. We call this force air pressure. *Air pressure*, then, can be defined simply as "the weight of the air per area of surface." At sea level, average air pressure is just slightly more than 1 kg per cm^2 (or approximately 14.7 lb per in.^{2}).

For a straw to work, there must be the force of air (air pressure) pushing down upon a liquid. When air is removed from the straw by sucking, it is this force that pushes the liquid up the straw to replace the removed air. With the unworkable straw, however, the liquid is not in contact with air—because the liquid completely fills the bottle, there is no air inside; and since the straw is sealed in the cap, the liquid is not in contact with room air. Thus sucking on the straw is to no avail. The straw works only when the cap is loosened, providing an access to air and the pressure it exerts.

PROCEDURE

Part One: Completing the Unworkable Straw

1. Distribute the materials to each student. Tell students that you want them each to make a special bottle for use in a science activity. Do not divulge the purpose of the bottle at this point.

2. Have students use strips of masking tape to attach identification labels to their bottles.

3. Instruct each student to insert the straw into the bottle cap so that the straw extends roughly halfway above the cap. They should each put the cap on the bottle to make sure there is clearance between the bottom of the straw and the bottom of the bottle. Then have each student remove the cap (with the inserted straw) from the bottle and place it on a paper towel.

4. Circulate among the students, placing a marble-sized glob of silicone sealant on each cap. Students should each completely seal the straw by working the sealant into and around the straw/cap intersection. Since it is critical that an airtight seal be achieved (the activity will not work without it), assist students with this step as necessary. You may wish to first demonstrate for the class by sealing one or two caps yourself.

5. After students have applied the sealant, have them wash their hands.

6. Have students each leave the cap/straw setup undisturbed on the toweling until the sealant has set enough to hold the straw in place when the cap is put onto the bottle—about an hour (see directions on the tube of sealant).

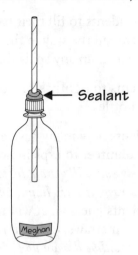

7. When the sealant has adequately set, instruct students to each place the cap on the bottle without screwing it down. They should then place the bottles in an area of the room where they will be out of the way until the sealant *fully* sets— about twenty-four hours (see directions on the tube of sealant).

(continues)

Part Two: The Unworkable Straw

1. When the sealant has completely set, have students retrieve their bottles.

2. Instruct students to fill their bottles completely with water—all the way to the rim, using paper towels to clean up any spills that result.

3. Ask students to tightly screw the cap/straw setups onto the bottles.

4. Ask students how many have ever used a straw. Invite a volunteer to explain how a straw works. *(Most likely you will get an answer such as: when you suck on a straw, it sucks liquid up the straw.)* Then have students guess what will happen when they suck on their straws. *(Most, if not all, will predict that water will be drawn up the straw.)*

5. Have students attempt to suck water out of their bottles through the straws. If the straw/cap seal is airtight, it will be impossible to do—much to their surprise! No matter how hard they suck, they will get no liquid or, at most, a drop or two. Ask students if they have any ideas as to why they all have unworkable straws.

6. Now tell students each to unscrew the cap, tilt it to one side (with the straw still in the bottle), and try again. This time each attempt will be successful.

7. Inquire once more as to why the straw did not work the first time. If necessary, lead students with questions such as:

   • What changed between the unsuccessful and the successful attempt? *(The cap was loosened and tilted to one side.)*

   • What did this allow that was prevented in the first try? *(It allowed air in the room to come in contact with the water in the bottle.)*

   • Why did this make the straw work?

8. Use the last question to discuss the role of air in the working of the straw, with the introduction of the concept of air pressure (see Teacher Information).

EXTENSIONS AND ADAPTATIONS

1. This activity is appropriate for use in a learning center.

2. Relate the results of this activity to the fact that most liquid storage cans (a gasoline can, for example) have two openings in them: one through which liquid can be poured out and one through which air can enter the can to help push the liquid out faster. Bring a clean gasoline can to class, fill it with water, and demonstrate the very different rates of flow with the air vent open versus closed.

3. Drill a hole in the bottom of a 2 L plastic soda bottle. Make the hole about 6 mm ($\frac{1}{4}$ in.) or so in diameter. (The plastic at the bottom of the bottle is thick and hard, but it is possible to punch with some effort, if you prefer to punch.) Hold a finger over the hole and fill the bottle with water. Keeping your finger over the hole, invert the bottle and have students time how long it takes for all the water to exit. Repeat the process. This time, however, remove your finger as you invert the bottle. The difference in exit times is tremendous.

4. Related activities Bag Pull on page 13, Marshmallow Mash on page 16, and I'm Under a Lot of Pressure on page 19.

BAG PULL

PRIMARY CONTENT

- Understanding the concept of air pressure
- Understanding the effect of a volume increase on air pressure
- Understanding that air moves from relatively higher pressure toward lower pressure

PRIOR STUDENT KNOWLEDGE

The concept of the molecular makeup of air

PRE-ACTIVITY PREPARATION

Each group will need a large wide-mouth jar. Plastic 1.13 kg (40 oz) peanut butter jars are perfect, and they are unbreakable; glass containers, such as mayonnaise jars, can also be used. Ask students to bring jars from home for use in the activity.

PROCESS SKILLS

Observing, inferring, hypothesizing, identifying variables, experimenting

GROUP SIZE

1–4 students

MATERIALS PER GROUP

- 1 suction cup, any type or size (may be separate or attached to a toy dart, for example) (for teacher use)
- 1 plastic fold-type sandwich bag (not the zip-lock type)
- 1 large wide-mouth jar
- 1 or 2 large, thick rubber bands
- 1 sheet of paper
- 1 pencil

TEACHER INFORMATION

Because of its molecular composition, air has weight or mass. As such, air exerts a force in all directions; this is referred to as air pressure. Air pressure is simply the weight of the air per area of surface. At sea level, average air pressure is just slightly more than 1 kg per cm² (or approximately 14.7 lb per in.²). In order to maintain air-pressure equilibrium, air moves from areas of relatively higher pressure (greater weight) toward areas of lower pressure (lesser weight). We refer to such movements of air as wind.

In the second part of this activity, the bag does move initially when pulled up. As the bag starts to move up, more space is made available inside the jar. Because the jar is sealed, no outside air can enter to fill this newly created space. Thus, the air in the jar will expand to fill the new space. This means that the same amount of air (the same weight) is now occupying a greater volume—the weight is spread over a greater area. As a result, the air pressure (weight per area) in the jar decreases, becoming lower than the air pressure outside the jar. Since air always moves from high pressure toward lower pressure, outside air tries to move into the jar. In this attempt, outside air pushes inward on the bag—to the point that students cannot overcome this inward-pushing weight. The result is that the bag cannot be removed from the jar until air is allowed into the jar (by releasing the seal or tearing the plastic) to increase the inside pressure.

A suction cup works on the principle of air pressure. As the cup is pushed in, it forces the inside air out. With little or no air inside the cup, the inside air pressure is very low. Outside air, in response, pushes in on the cup, keeping it in place.

PROCEDURE

1. If necessary, review with students the fact that air is composed of molecules and thus has weight and occupies a space. Also review the fluid nature of air—that air flows and takes the shape of its container.

2. Introduce this activity by showing the class a suction cup. Wet the cup and stick it onto a smooth surface. Ask students if they have any ideas about why or how a suction cup works. Listen to responses but do not provide answers or content material at this time.

3. Inform the class that today's activity may help answer the previous question.

4. Group students and distribute the materials. Provide groups with instructions as delineated in steps 5–13.

5. Have students blow some air into the sandwich bag to open it up and then slide the opening of the bag over the outside of the jar's mouth—like putting a glove (the bag) on a hand (the jar). They should then pull the bag down over the jar for a distance of about 2.5 cm (1 in.) or so (see illustration).

6. Ask students to seal the bag to the jar by wrapping a rubber band tightly around the bag and the lip of the jar several times. It is important that an airtight seal be achieved. (Assist groups with this step as necessary.)

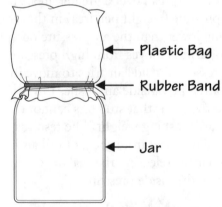

Plastic Bag
Rubber Band
Jar

7. Have groups each develop and record on a sheet of paper a prediction as to what will happen when they attempt to push the bag into the jar. (Ask groups to share their predictions, and the reasoning for such, with the class.)

8. Now have groups push the bags into the jars. Ask them to be sure to only push gently on the bags so they don't tear the plastic. (As long as the plastic is not torn, students cannot push the bags into the jars.)

9. Ask, "Why were you unable to push the bags into the jars?" *(If they knew that air occupies space, students should have predicted this result. Because the jar is already filled with air, and because of the airtight seal that prevents air from escaping the jar, the plastic bag and the air that it contains cannot also occupy the jar—two things cannot occupy the same space at the same time.)*

10. Have groups carefully remove the rubber bands and bags from the jars.

11. Then have each group again blow into the bag to open it up. This time have students insert the bag (open end up) inside the jar so that it hangs full length, leaving about 2.5 cm (1 in.) of the bag sticking out of the top of the jar. Ask students to fold this excess over the jar's rim and secure it tightly with a rubber band as previously (see illustration). It is important that an airtight seal be achieved. (Assist groups with this step as necessary.)

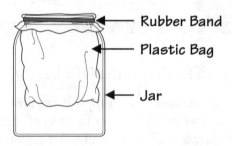

Rubber Band
Plastic Bag
Jar

12. Point out to groups that in the previous part of the activity, they couldn't push the bags into the jars. Ask if they think that this time they will be able to pull the bag out of the jar. Have them develop and record on the paper a prediction as to what will happen when they attempt to pull the bag out of the jar. (Ask each group to share their prediction and the reasoning for it with the class.)

13. Have students in each group reach inside the jar (and bag), grasp the bottom of the bag, and gently pull upward. Group members should take turns so that each student gets to try the bag pull. Caution students not to pull so hard that they tear the bag! (As long as the plastic is not torn, students will not be able to pull the bags out of the jars!)

14. Conduct a session to discuss the students' lack of success at the bag pull. Present explanations and content material as necessary, including the concept of air pressure and the response of air to differences in air pressure (see Teacher Information).

15. Conclude the activity by asking students if they can now infer how a suction cup works (see Teacher Information).

EXTENSIONS AND ADAPTATIONS

1. This activity is appropriate for use in a learning center.

2. Bring a fireplace bellows to class. Using the smoke from a match or a Fourth of July punk, show students how air enters the bellows when the bellows is opened or expanded. Relate the opening of the bellows to the "pulling up" on the bag in the jar in the primary activity—an expansion of volume and lowering of inside air pressure. As air moves toward lower pressure, there is an opening that allows air to enter the bellows; with the jar and bag, however, there was not!

3. Fill a plastic glass completely full of water—all the way to the rim. Place an index card over the top of the glass. While holding the card in place, invert the glass. Remove your hand. The card stays on the inverted opening and no water spills out! (Do this over a sink or pail just in case.) The air pressure exerted up on the card is greater than the pressure exerted down on the card by the water. Thus the card stays put against the glass.

4. Related activities Balloon Kebab on page 2, Unworkable Straw on page 10, Marshmallow Mash on page 16, and I'm Under a Lot of Pressure on page 19.

MARSHMALLOW MASH _____

PRIMARY CONTENT
- Understanding the effect of volume increases and decreases on air pressure
- Understanding that air moves from relatively higher pressure toward lower pressure

PRIOR STUDENT KNOWLEDGE
Exposure to the concept of air pressure and the movement of air associated with differences in air pressure; suggested completion of the activity Bag Pull on page 13

PRE-ACTIVITY PREPARATION
Each group will need a plastic syringe (the type used to orally administer medicine to small animals or children—the type of syringe without a needle). The size of the syringe is not critical as long as the tube is large enough so that a miniature marshmallow can be easily dropped (not forced) into it. Plastic syringes are not expensive and you can purchase them at many farm supply stores, pet shops, drugstores, hardware stores, or home-supply stores. If tip protectors or caps are on the syringes, remove them prior to the activity.

PROCESS SKILLS
Observing, comparing, inferring, hypothesizing, identifying variables, experimenting

GROUP SIZE
1–3 students

MATERIALS PER GROUP
- 1 plastic syringe
- 1 miniature marshmallow
- 1 regular-sized marshmallow (for teacher use)

TEACHER INFORMATION

As air expands (undergoes a volume increase), its weight is distributed over a greater area. Consequently, air pressure (weight per area) decreases. When air contracts (undergoes a volume decrease), its weight is concentrated into a smaller area. The result is that air pressure increases. In response to differences in air pressure, air always moves from areas of relatively higher pressure toward areas of lower pressure—

this is the primary cause of winds. In this activity, students alter the air pressure within a plastic syringe by changing the position of the plunger which, in turn, changes the volume of the air. Students are then able to visibly observe the effects of changing air pressure on air movement by seeing a marshmallow within the syringe significantly expand and contract in size. This activity has proven to be a real favorite among students.

PROCEDURE

1. If necessary, review with students the basic concepts of air pressure and air movement in response to differences in air pressure.

2. Introduce this activity by showing students the regular-sized marshmallow. Inform them that marshmallows all have quite a bit of air trapped (as tiny air bubbles) among their ingredients. Ask students if they can think of a way to use the concept of air pressure to show that air is trapped in a marshmallow. After students have debated the question, tell them that they will try out one way in today's activity.

3. Group students and distribute the materials. Provide groups with instructions as delineated in steps 4–7. Assure students that they will each get their turn working with the syringe; as each student takes a turn, other group members should closely observe results.

4. Have a student in each group pull the plunger completely out of the syringe tube, drop 1 miniature marshmallow into the tube, and reinsert the plunger to a position about one-fourth of the way down the tube. Ask, "Does that part of the tube below the plunger presently contain anything besides a marshmallow?" (*Yes, it is also filled with air.* Make sure all students reach this conclusion.)

5. The same student in each group should take the syringe in one hand and put a finger of that hand tightly over the opening (tip) to totally block it. This leaves the other hand free to operate the plunger. Keeping the finger tight against the opening, have the student push the plunger down as far as he/she can (without smashing the marshmallow!) and observe the marshmallow. Ask questions such as the following:

   - What happened to the space that the air occupied (its volume) as the plunger was pushed down? (*As the plunger was pushed down, the air in the tube was compacted into a smaller space or volume.*)

   - Did this decrease in volume change the air pressure inside the tube? How? (*Yes; air pressure in the tube increased. The original amount of air [the original weight] was now occupying a smaller volume, that is, the weight was concentrated over a smaller area. As a result, the air pressure [weight per area] in the tube increased.*)

   - What did you observe that proved that air pressure in the tube increased? Why? (*The marshmallow shrank in size! As air pressure in the tube increased, it caused an increase in the force (weight) pushing in on the marshmallow. The marshmallow responded by compacting under the greater pressure.*)

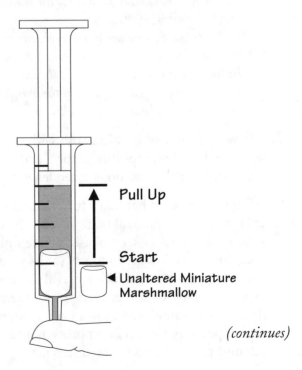

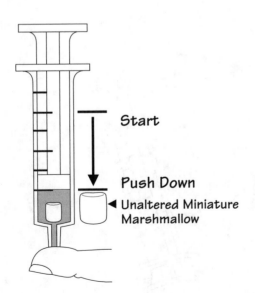

(continues)

6. Have each student remove his/her finger from the opening and then push the plunger down the tube to the point that it is just above the marshmallow, being careful not to smash the marshmallow. Have them each again tightly block the syringe opening and then slowly pull the plunger up to the top of the tube, being careful not to pull the plunger completely out of the tube! Have each group observe the marshmallow. Ask questions such as the following:

   • What happened to the space that the air occupied (its volume) as the plunger was pulled up? *(As the plunger was pulled up, the air in the tube expanded to fill the newly created space—the volume of the air was increased.)*

   • Did this increase in volume change the air pressure inside the tube? How? *(Yes; air pressure in the tube decreased. The original amount of air [the original weight] was now occupying a greater volume, that is, the weight was spread over a greater area. As a result, the air pressure [weight per area] in the tube decreased.)*

   • What did you observe that proved that air pressure in the tube decreased? Does this show that a marshmallow has air in it? *(The marshmallow enlarged to a size much bigger than normal! As air pressure in the tube decreased, it became lower than the pressure of air trapped inside the marshmallow. Since air moves from higher toward lower air pressure, the air in the marshmallow tried to move out into the tube. Because the air is trapped within the marshmallow, this outward movement [within the marshmallow] caused the marshmallow to swell.)*

7. Allow each student to take a turn with the syringe and marshmallow, repeating steps 5 and 6 each time (without the questioning sequence).

8. After each student has had a turn shrinking and enlarging the marshmallow, review results of the activity with the class, emphasizing the following relationships: (a) as air contracts (as its volume decreases), air pressure increases; (b) as air expands (as its volume increases), air pressure decreases; (c) air always moves from relatively higher pressure toward lower pressure in an attempt to equalize pressure differences.

EXTENSIONS AND ADAPTATIONS

1. This activity is appropriate for use in a learning center.

2. Provide students with additional marshmallows and let them experiment on their own with the relationships identified in Procedure step 8.

3. Have a contest to see which group or student can get a marshmallow to enlarge to the greatest size and shrink to the smallest size.

4. Related activities Balloon Kebab on page 2, Unworkable Straw on page 10, Bag Pull on page 13, and I'm Under a Lot of Pressure on page 19.

I'M UNDER A LOT OF PRESSURE

PRIMARY CONTENT

- Understanding the effect of temperature changes on air pressure in a closed environment
- Understanding that air moves from relatively higher pressure toward lower pressure

PRIOR STUDENT KNOWLEDGE

Exposure to the concept of air pressure and the movement of air associated with differences in air pressure; suggested completion of the activity Bag Pull on page 13

PRE-ACTIVITY PREPARATION

No special pre-activity preparation is required.

PROCESS SKILLS

Observing, inferring, identifying variables

GROUP SIZE

Whole class

MATERIALS PER GROUP

- 1 large container with transparent sides (plastic sweater box or aquarium tank, for example), large enough so that you can immerse a 2 L soda bottle in it (for teacher demonstration)
- 1 plastic soda bottle, 2 L, label removed, with cap, (for teacher demonstration)
- 1 cooler with cubed or crushed ice (for teacher demonstration)
- Available water (for teacher demonstration)
- Very hot tap water and a container with at least a 473 mL (16 oz) capacity OR a hot plate and pan with a similar capacity that can be used for heating water (for teacher demonstration)
- 1 funnel (for teacher demonstration)

TEACHER INFORMATION

In this activity, air pressure is altered primarily through a change in temperature of air in a closed container (a 2 L bottle). When air in the bottle is heated by the addition of hot water, the air molecules move more rapidly. Each time an air molecule hits the wall of the container, pressure is exerted upon the container. Consequently, the more frequently the molecules strike (the higher the temperature), the greater the inside air pressure. With inside air pressure higher now than outside air pressure, air in the bottle tries to move outward toward the lower pressure. The bottle walls, however, are not outwardly flexible and little evidence of this outward push is seen.

When the bottle is immersed in cold water, the temperature of the inside air is decreased drastically, with a corresponding decrease in molecular motion. Since the molecules are now moving much slower, they strike the bottle walls much less frequently. The result is a significant decrease in air pressure, to the point where the inside air pressure becomes much lower than the outside air pressure. Since air moves from higher toward lower pressure, the outside air pushes strongly inward on the bottle. The bottle sides are inwardly flexible, and they respond by crushing and deforming inwardly.

(continues)

(continued)

The effect of temperature on air pressure can be somewhat confusing. In a closed environment (such as the bottle), an increase in temperature causes an increase in air pressure and vice versa (a direct relationship). In an open, uncontained environment (such as the atmosphere), on the other hand, an increase in temperature causes increased volume and decreased air pressure; and a decrease in temperature results in decreased volume and increased pressure (an inverse relationship). Whether you choose to expose your students at this time to these two different effects of temperature upon pressure (depending on whether the environment is contained or uncontained) depends on your objectives.

PROCEDURE

1. If necessary, review with students the basic concept of air pressure and the movement of air in response to differences in air pressure.

2. Ask students if they know what can cause a change in air pressure. (If students have completed the activity Bag Pull on page 13, they should be aware that changes in the amount of space occupied by the air [its volume] will result in changes in air pressure.)

3. Ask the class if they can think of anything else that might cause air pressure to change, especially in a confined environment (air in a closed container, for example). Students will probably mention temperature sooner or later; when they do, suggest an experiment to investigate that possibility. If they don't mention temperature, use leading questions until they suggest it.

4. Have students gather around your work area so that everyone can view the demonstration.

5. Fill the large container about half to three-fourths full with water—enough so that you can immerse the 2 L bottle. Add plenty of ice to the water—the colder the water, the better.

6. Insert the funnel into the mouth of the 2 L plastic bottle. Ask students why the bottle is not being crushed inward by the air pressure in the room. *(There is also air filling the bottle, and since the bottle is open to the room, air can easily pass between the two. As a result, the pressure of the air in the bottle pushing out on the bottle sides is equal to the air pressure in the room pushing in on the bottle sides.)*

7. Obtain approximately 473 mL (16 oz) of very hot tap water. If your tap water does not get exceptionally hot, you will obtain better results if you heat that amount of water on a hot plate. CAUTION: If you heat the water on a hot plate, be careful not to let it get too hot—certainly not to boiling! Approximately the temperature of a hot cup of coffee will be enough. If the water is too hot, it can soften the plastic bottle.

8. Pour the hot water into the bottle through the funnel. Remove the funnel and swish the hot water around inside the bottle. Ask students what the water is doing to the temperature of the air inside the bottle. *(The hot water is heating the air inside the bottle.)*

9. After ten or fifteen seconds of swishing, pour the hot water back into its original container and immediately screw the cap tightly on the bottle to separate the air in the bottle from the air in the room.

10. Tell students to watch and listen. Then immerse the bottle in the container of ice-cold water. Students will see and hear the bottle sides collapsing and crunching inward! It's really exciting. Keep the bottle in the water until all deformation ceases (a minute or two).

11. Remove the bottle and place it on the table. The bottle will look even more deformed out of the water.

12. Discuss the results of the activity. Include questions such as:

- What happened to the air temperature in the bottle when I immersed it in cold water? *(The air temperature inside the bottle dropped a great deal.)*

- What happened to the bottle when I put it in the cold water? *(It crushed inward.)*

- How did the air pressure inside the bottle compare to the air pressure in the room after I put the bottle in the cold water? *(The air pressure inside the bottle became much lower than the air pressure in the room.)*

- How do you know? *(The bottle crushed inward; air moves from relatively higher pressure toward lower pressure. The pressure inside the bottle must have been lower than outside, causing air to push [move] inward against the sides of the bottle, crushing it.)*

- Then what does a temperature decrease do to the pressure of air in a closed container? *(As temperature decreases, pressure decreases.)*

- What do you think a temperature increase does to the pressure of air in a closed container? *(As temperature increases, pressure increases.)*

- If the pressure got higher when the air was heated, why didn't the bottle bend outward? *(While the bottle sides can bend inward, they are too rigid to expand outward very much.)*

13. Discuss with students why temperature affects pressure as it does in a closed container (see Teacher Information). Ask students if they can think of actual examples where this relationship is observed. This may prove difficult for students at this level, but two examples with which some students might be familiar are:

a. Tires tend to get soft and underinflated during very cold weather even though they are not leaking air. Likewise, tires will become overinflated in very hot weather. Students may have noticed this on bicycle tires.

b. Students may have watched food being prepared with a pressure cooker. If so, they might have noticed that the gauge shows an increase in pressure while the cooker is being heated. After the cooker is removed from the heat and begins to cool, the gauge shows a decrease in pressure. Also, during heating, the cooker gives off steam, an indication that air is moving from high pressure inside the cooker to lower pressure outside.

EXTENSIONS AND ADAPTATIONS

1. Repeat the activity. This time, instead of immersing the capped bottle in cold water, just set it on the table and let students observe. The air inside will still cool—just not as fast or as much. As the air cools, the bottle will deform inward, sometimes more noisily than in the water. While not as great as in the water, the deformation of the bottle will be significant; and students enjoy watching it crush-in gradually while it just sits there.

2. Bring a pressure cooker and hot plate to class. Demonstrate for students the example given in Procedure step 13b.

3. Related activities Balloon Kebab on page 2, Unworkable Straw on page 10, Bag Pull on page 13, and Marshmallow Mash on page 16.

RECORD A TEMP

PRIMARY CONTENT

- Understanding the operation of a thermometer
- Recording and graphing daily temperatures
- Interpreting temperature trends

PRIOR STUDENT KNOWLEDGE

The ability to read a thermometer; experience with graphing

PRE-ACTIVITY PREPARATION

1. Using the reproducible Daily Temperature Chart (page 25) as a guide, construct a large, classroom-size daily temperature chart on poster board. You can indicate the days of the month numerically in the small upper-left boxes of the chart.
2. Copy reproducibles Daily Temperature Chart (page 25) and Daily Temperature Graph (page 26), one copy of each per student.

PROCESS SKILLS

Observing, comparing, inferring, measuring, recording data, communicating

GROUP SIZE

Whole class

MATERIALS PER GROUP

- 1 classroom-size daily temperature chart (see Pre-Activity Preparation)
- 1 Fahrenheit thermometer
- 1 copy of reproducible Daily Temperature Chart for each student
- 1 copy of reproducible Daily Temperature Graph for each student

TEACHER INFORMATION

A thermometer is an instrument used to measure air temperature. Inside the thermometer bulb is liquid (mercury or alcohol). When the liquid is heated through conduction with warmer air, the liquid will expand and rise in the tube. When the liquid is cooled by conductive loss of heat to cooler surrounding air, the liquid will contract and fall.

The primary control of air temperature at a given location is the amount of solar energy received at that location. There are, however, a number of secondary controls that may cause the temperature to deviate. Examples of such deviations include: an unusually warm day in winter or cold day in summer, the high for the day occurring in the morning rather than in the afternoon, and temperatures near buildings being different than temperatures in the open. Because of such secondary influences, seasonal trends in temperature (such as the cooling with approaching winter or the warming with approaching summer) often do not show up on day-to-day temperature comparisons but become apparent only with longer-term observations of a month or more. It is also because of secondary influences that daily temperature measurements should be taken at the same location and the same time each day.

Saturdays and Sundays create an apparent problem in activities such as this one which require extended temperature observations. Neither you nor your students are present at school on these days to take the temperature readings. Actually, this turns out to be a benefit rather than a problem because it illustrates an occurrence typical in many scientific investigations at the professional level. For a multitude of reasons, scientists often experience missing data in their research. Sometimes the problem can be handled using statistical techniques; at other times, different approaches are called for. In this activity, it is recommended that weekend data be handled in one of two ways:

1. You can fill in Saturdays and Sundays with media-reported temperatures for the appropriate time of day. While some difference is likely, these temperatures will probably be fairly close to those at the school site.

2. Less preferably, you can leave the weekends as missing data. In this case, Friday's and Monday's points on the graph would not be connected, resulting in a discontinuous line.

PROCEDURE

1. Introduce the activity by asking students questions such as the following, presenting explanations as necessary:

   - What instrument is used to tell how warm or cold the air is? *(thermometer)*

   - If we wanted to compare the temperatures taken on thirty different days, how could we remember what the temperatures were each of those days? *(The data would have to be recorded; recording data assists the recall and organization of the data.)*

   - If only one temperature reading is taken on each of those thirty days, should we take the temperature at the same time each day? Why? (see Teacher Information)

   - Should we take the temperature at the same location each day for a fair comparison? Why? (see Teacher Information)

2. Tell students that they are going to be meteorologists (scientists who study the weather) during the next month—taking, recording, and examining air temperature on a daily basis.

3. Display and explain the classroom chart that students will use for recording daily temperatures. Include an explanation as to how they will handle the missing data for Saturdays and Sundays (see Teacher Information). Indicate that you will give all students a Daily Temperature Chart so that they can each keep their own record of the temperature changes.

4. Show students the thermometer that they will use in the activity. Discuss with them how to properly use a thermometer to take temperature readings. Explicitly warn them against touching the thermometer bulb.

(continues)

(continued)

5. Give each student a Daily Temperature Chart. Tell them that they are to copy the dates shown on the classroom chart.

6. Select two different students each day to take the thermometer outdoors and measure the air temperature at the same time and in the same place. If available, a shaded location will provide the most accurate readings. Students should allow the thermometer time to adjust to the outdoor temperature prior to making the reading (about two or three minutes).

7. The returning students should share the temperature reading with the class and record the temperature on the class chart. Class members should then record the temperature reading on their individual temperature charts.

8. At the end of the month, distribute a Daily Temperature Graph to each student. Have each graph their data in line-graph format. Assist students with graphing and with reading the labels on the graph, as necessary. Ask students to explain the advantage of graphing the information. *(Graphs aid in the interpretation of data because trends and changes become visually apparent.)*

9. Conduct a discussion of the chart and graph results. Include questions such as:

   • What does this information tell us?

   • On what day did we get the lowest reading?

   • On what day did we get the highest reading?

   • Why do weather forecasters keep records of the temperature for a long time? *(to be able to see general trends or patterns in the weather;* see Teacher Information*)*

   • Do you see any trends in our data? If so, what kind? What do they mean or suggest?

   • Compare the first week in the month to the last week. Are there major differences?

EXTENSIONS AND ADAPTATIONS

1. Have students record the morning and evening temperatures at home for two weeks. If a thermometer is not available at home, they may use local media reports. Have students record and graph their findings and discuss the results in class (morning-to-evening, day-to-day, week-to-week, and unusual trends, for example).

2. Have students keep a record of the daily temperature (at a given time) for several months. Decide if any observable trends or patterns are present.

3. Have students use local media forecasts and data as a source to keep a record of the predicted and actual daily high (or low) temperature for a period of time. Let students compare the results and judge the accuracy of the predictions.

4. Related activities Time Is Energy on page 27 and How Hot Is It? on page 32.

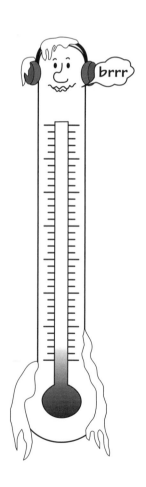

RECORD A TEMP

DAILY TEMPERATURE CHART

Name _____

MONTH _____

High Temperature for Month _____   Low Temperature for Month _____

SUNDAY	MONDAY	TUESDAY	WEDNESDAY	THURSDAY	FRIDAY	SATURDAY

Earth Science Activities (KSAM)

RECORD A TEMP

DAILY TEMPERATURE GRAPH

Name

MONTH

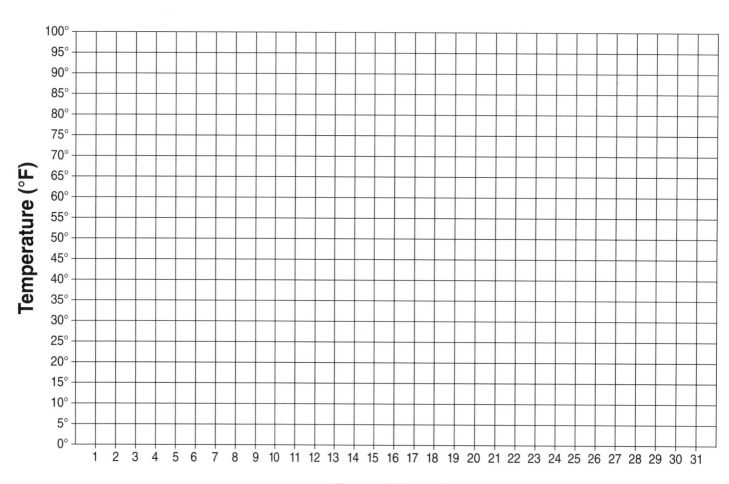

TIME IS ENERGY

PRIMARY CONTENT
Understanding the relationship between color, energy absorption, and temperature

PRIOR STUDENT KNOWLEDGE
The ability to read a thermometer; experience with graphing

PRE-ACTIVITY PREPARATION
1. Obtain a dark colored T-shirt and a white T-shirt (or some other article of unisex clothing).
2. Copy reproducibles Student Data Table (page 30) and Student Temperature Graphs (page 31), one copy per student.
3. For best results, do the activity on a bright, sunny day.

PROCESS SKILLS
Observing, comparing, inferring, measuring, recording data, communicating, hypothesizing, experimenting

GROUP SIZE
2–4 students

MATERIALS PER GROUP
- 2 identical clear plastic cups, 177 mL (6 oz) or larger capacity
- Available water (for whole class)
- food coloring (dark red or blue)
- 1 plastic spoon
- 1 sheet of paper
- 1 pencil
- 2 thermometers
- 1 copy of reproducible Student Data Table for each student
- 1 copy of reproducible Student Temperature Graphs for each student

TEACHER INFORMATION

The temperature attained by a given material is a function of the amount of heat energy that is absorbed by that material—the greater the amount of energy absorption, the higher the temperature. The amount of energy absorption is affected by several factors, one of the most important being the color of the material. Dark colors absorb energy much more effectively than do light colors, which tend to reflect the energy. Generally speaking, the darker the color, the greater the absorption rate. Thus dark-colored materials not only tend to heat up faster than light-colored materials, they also usually reach a higher temperature. This relationship between color and temperature has many practical applications, only a very few of which are implied in step 12 of the Procedure.

PROCEDURE

1. Introduce the activity by showing the class the dark-colored and white T-shirts (or other articles of unisex clothing). Ask questions such as the following but do not provide answers at this time:

   - Pretend that it is very hot outside and you are going to watch a baseball game. You will be sitting in the uncovered bleachers. Which one of these T-shirts would you wear to stay the coolest, or would it not make any difference?

   - Pretend that you are going to watch a football game. It looks nice and warm out, so you decide to wear a T-shirt. After you've been outside for awhile, you realize that it is cooler than you had thought. Which one of these T-shirts would keep you the warmest, or would it not make any difference?

   - Do you think the color of a material affects how warm the material gets when it is exposed to heat?

2. Tell students that in today's activity they will learn the answers to these questions by measuring temperatures of clear water and dark-colored water.

3. Group students and distribute the materials. If necessary, review with students how to use a thermometer to take temperature readings.

4. Instruct each group to fill both of their cups about three-quarters full with water. If students will be getting their water from a tap, have them use the cold-water tap. Let it run a minute or two before students begin filling to allow the water temperature to stabilize. Then let it run continually until all groups have obtained their water.

5. Tell groups that the amounts of water in their 2 cups must be equal. Have them sit their 2 cups side-by-side and compare water levels, making adjustments as necessary.

6. Have each group add dark food coloring to one of their cups of water, stirring it to mix. It is important that this water be deeply colored.

7. Direct each group to develop a prediction as to whether there will be a temperature difference between the 2 cups of water after both are exposed to direct sunlight and if so, which temperature will be higher and why. Ask each group to record its prediction on a sheet of paper.

8. Groups should now place their cups in a location where the cups will be exposed to direct sunlight (either indoors or outdoors if conditions allow). They should also place a thermometer in each cup.

9. To give the thermometers time to adjust, have each group wait about one minute before taking their starting temperature reading (0 minutes). After this first reading, groups should take and record the temperature every two minutes. Each group member should record the data for the group in the Data Table on the Student Data Table. (Note: The data table and graphs allow the investigation to continue for forty-five minutes. However, significant temperature differences may become apparent within twenty to thirty minutes. If so, you can shorten this activity.)

10. At the end of the data acquisition period, each student is to display the data for the 2 cups in line graphs on the reproducible Student Temperature Graphs. If students are not yet comfortable with line graphs, have them display the data in bar graphs. Assist students with reading the labels on the data table and temperature graphs as necessary.

11. Conduct a session to review and discuss results, presenting explanations and additional content material where appropriate. Include questions such as:

- What was your highest recorded temperature for the clear water? *(Specific results will vary, but the temperature of the clear water will normally be lower than that of the dark water.)*

- What was your highest recorded temperature for the dark water? *(Specific results will vary, but the temperature of the dark water will normally be higher than that of the clear water.)*

- So which of the two samples reached the highest temperature? *(normally, the dark water)*

- Based on your graphs, did the temperatures increase in the 2 cups at the same rate or speed? *(Normally, temperatures will increase faster in the dark water, indicated on the graph by a more steeply sloping line.)*

- So does the color of a material affect both the rate (speed) and the amount that it heats? *(yes)*

- Why do you think this happens? (see Teacher Information)

12. Check comprehension of the discussed relationships by presenting situations such as the following:

- Which would keep you cooler on a hot day, a white T-shirt or a purple T-shirt? *(white)*

- Which would keep you warmer on a cold day, a yellow coat or a red coat? *(red)*

- If you lived where it was very cold, which would keep your house warmer, a roof with black shingles or a roof with light gray shingles? *(black)* White siding on a house or brown siding? *(brown)*

- If you lived where it was very hot, which would keep your house cooler, a roof with red shingles or a roof with light gray shingles? *(light gray)* Yellow siding on the house or blue siding? *(yellow)*

EXTENSIONS AND ADAPTATIONS

1. This activity is appropriate for use in a learning center.

2. If you used both red and blue food coloring for the dark color in the activity, compare results for those two colors. Was there a consistent difference between the two in terms of heating characteristics?

3. Repeat the activity using a variety of colors. Then have students rank-order the colors in terms of the highest temperature reached.

4. Take the students out on a sunny day and measure the temperatures about one inch above blacktop or asphalt surfaces and about one inch above concrete surfaces; compare the two.

5. Related activities Record a Temp on page 22 and How Hot Is It? on page 32.

TIME IS ENERGY

STUDENT DATA TABLE

Name

DATA TABLE

Time (min)	Temperature	
	Clear Water	Dark Water
0		
5		
10		
15		
20		
25		
30		
35		
40		
45		

Earth Science Activities (KSAM)

TIME IS ENERGY

STUDENT TEMPERATURE GRAPHS

Name

Container with Clear Water

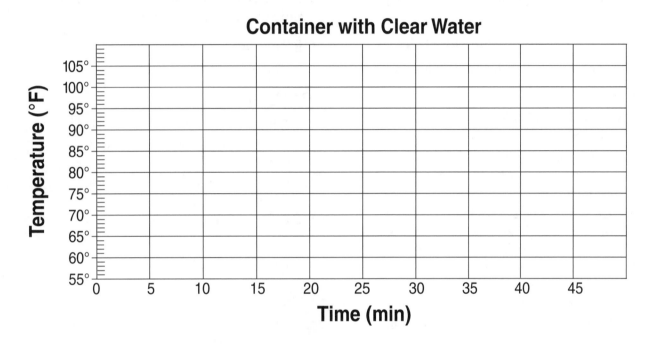

Container with Dark-Colored Water

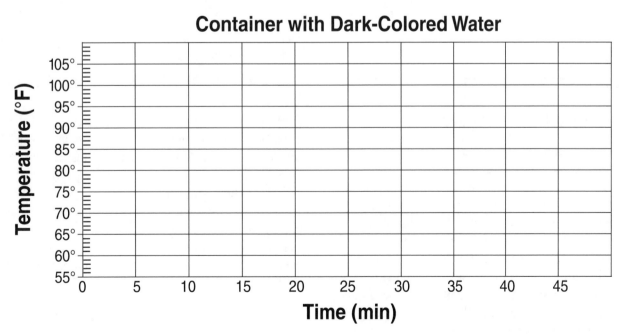

HOW HOT IS IT? _____

PRIMARY CONTENT

Understanding the differential heating of land and water and the effects of such differences on climate

PRIOR STUDENT KNOWLEDGE

The ability to read a thermometer; previous graphing experience

PRE-ACTIVITY PREPARATION

1. Obtain a bag of topsoil from any garden supply center and leave the soil out in the classroom overnight to attain room temperature.
2. Each group will need 355 mL (12 oz) of room-temperature water. Fill enough 3.79 L (1 gal) milk jugs with water to provide the amount needed. Leave the water out in the classroom overnight to attain room temperature.
3. Copy reproducible Student Data Sheet (page 35), one copy per student.
4. Do this activity on a bright, sunny day.

PROCESS SKILLS

Observing, comparing, inferring, measuring, recording, data, communicating, hypothesizing, identifying variables, experimenting

GROUP SIZE

2–4 students

MATERIALS PER GROUP

- 1 map of the United States (for whole class)
- 1 bag of room-temperature topsoil (for whole class)
- Container(s) of room-temperature water (for whole class)
- 2 opaque plastic cups, 473 mL (16 oz)
- 2 rulers
- 1 paper towel
- 2 erasers
- Transparent tape
- 2 thermometers
- 1 copy of reproducible Student Data Sheet for each student
- Red and blue markers or colored pencils for each student

TEACHER INFORMATION

Other factors being equal, soil heats and cools faster than does an equal volume of water; and soil reaches more extreme temperatures. This is why soil is warm enough for spring gardening and planting long before swimming pools are warm enough for swimming. There are a number of reasons for the differential heating and cooling characteristics of soil and water. Some of the most important are as follows. (a) Water is transparent or translucent, while soil is opaque. This causes energy to concentrate at the top of the soil, while energy is distributed to a greater depth in water.

(b) Water reflects more energy than does soil. Energy must be absorbed, not reflected, to heat a material. (c) Water is a fluid and circulates, thus distributing the heat energy throughout. Since there is no circulation in soil, the energy stays more concentrated. (d) Water has a higher specific heat than does soil. This means it takes more heat energy to raise 1 g of water 1° Celsius than it does 1 g of soil. (e) More evaporation occurs over water which, in turn, affects the heating and cooling rates.

Climate can be greatly affected by the fact that land goes to temperature extremes, while water stays more moderate. Even though they are located at about the same latitude, San Francisco has cooler summers (July average of about 63° F) and milder winters (January average of about 49° F) than does St. Louis which has hotter summers (July average of about 80° F) and colder winters (January average of about 29° F). Since most of the United States is in the Prevailing Westerly wind belt, San Francisco's location puts it on our windward coast. Its climate is dominated by winds that have crossed the Pacific Ocean, with the ocean's moderating effect on temperature. By the time those winds reach St. Louis, they have traveled across a large expanse of land, which transfers its more extreme temperatures to the winds. The result is hotter summers and colder winters for residents of St. Louis. Despite their coastal location, cities on the east coast do not benefit much from the moderating effects of the Atlantic because the westerly winds that affect them are coming off the continent, not off the ocean.

PROCEDURE

1. Introduce the activity by displaying a map of the United States and showing students the locations of San Francisco and St. Louis. Point out that both cities are located at about the same latitude.

2. Ask students to guess which of the two cities has hotter summers—or do they think that the summers in both places are about the same? Tally guesses on the board. Repeat the question with reference to colder winters; again tally the responses.

3. Inform the class that St. Louis has significantly hotter summers and colder winters than does San Francisco. Ask students if they can think of a reason why two places at essentially the same latitude would have such different summer temperatures and such different winter temperatures.

4. As students look at the map and consider the question, inevitably the influence of water on San Francisco's temperature will be among the ideas that they suggest—based on the fact that San Francisco is in a coastal location and St. Louis is not. Indicate that the best way to determine whether water heats and cools differently than land does is through an investigation.

5. Group students and distribute the materials. Point out the bag of topsoil and the container(s) of water. Provide groups with instructions as delineated in steps 6–13.

6. Have each group add room-temperature water to one cup until the cup is about $\frac{3}{4}$ full and then measure the depth of the water by inserting a ruler vertically into the cup. Then ask students to remove the ruler from the first cup and to stand another (dry) ruler in the second cup. To the second cup, students should add soil, tamping it down lightly until the soil is at the same depth as the water. Students can now withdraw the ruler and clean and dry both rulers with a paper towel.

7. As illustrated, ask each group to tape an eraser to the top side of a ruler at about the midway point so that one edge of the eraser is even with one edge of the ruler. They should now set the ruler atop the cup of water.

8. Have each group hold the back side of a thermometer against the edge of the eraser/ruler, move the thermometer up or down until its bulb is about 1.3 cm ($\frac{1}{2}$ in.) below the water surface and then tape the thermometer to the edge of the eraser. Students should then position the ruler so that the thermometer is at the center of the cup (see illustration).

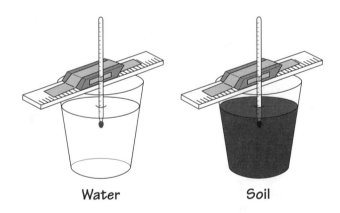

Water   Soil

9. Ask each group to repeat steps 7 and 8 to make an identical set up for the cup containing soil (see illustration).

(continues)

(continued)

10. Have students carefully move both cups to a location where the cups are exposed to direct sunlight. As soon as the cups are in position, students in each group should take the first temperature reading of the soil and the water and record those readings in the 0 (start) time row on the Data Table on the Student Data Sheet.

11. Have each group observe and record temperatures of the two materials again after five, ten, and fifteen minutes. This is the heating stage of the experiment.

12. Immediately after the fifteen-minute reading has been made, ask each group to carefully move both cups to a shaded location. Students should continue observing and recording temperatures at twenty, twenty-five, and thirty minutes. This is the cooling stage of the experiment.

13. At the conclusion of the observations, instruct students to each plot their data in a line graph on the Temperature Graph on the Student Data Sheet. They should draw the soil line in red and the water line in blue. Assist students with labeling the temperatures on the vertical axis of the provided graph—values have not been included in order to allow for the use of either Celsius or Fahrenheit thermometers.

14. Conduct a session to review and discuss results. Include questions such as:

    • What was the highest temperature reached by the soil during the heating stage of the experiment? The water? *(Results will vary.)*

    • Which material warmed to a higher temperature? *(Soil will attain a higher temperature than water, other factors being equal.)*

    • Look at your graph. Which material heated at a faster rate? *(Other factors being equal, the soil will have heated at a faster rate, as indicated by a steeper graph line)*

    • What was the temperature of the soil at the end of the cooling period? The water? *(Results will vary.)*

    • Which material cooled to a lower temperature? *(Other factors being equal, the soil will have cooled to a lower temperature than the water.)*

    • Which material cooled at a faster rate? *(Other factors being equal, the soil will have cooled at a faster rate.)*

    • Can you think of any reasons (variables) why specific temperatures were not the same among the samples of all the groups in the class? *(Examples include: differences in location and depth of the thermometer, differences in starting temperatures, and reader error.)*

    • Why do you think soil heats and cools differently than does water? (See Teacher Information)

15. Discuss with the class how differential heating of land and water, combined with the direction of the prevailing winds, explains why St. Louis has extreme summers and winters but San Francisco has moderate summers and winters, while both are at approximately the same latitude (see Teacher Information).

EXTENSIONS AND ADAPTATIONS

1. This activity is suitable for use in a learning center.

2. To obtain greater differences in the heating and cooling of soil and water, extend the length of the activity to include six heating and six cooling observations, all at five-minute intervals.

3. Rather than using solar energy, you can obtain greater differences by using either heat lamps or work lights as the energy source. Position each about 30.5 cm (12 in.) above the cups.

4. If necessary, you can also do this activity as a whole-class activity, using just one setup.

5. Related activities Record a Temp on page 22 and Time Is Energy on page 27.

HOW HOT IS IT? _____

STUDENT DATA SHEET

Name_____

Data Table

	Time (min)	TEMPERATURE	
		Soil	Water
Heating	0 (start)		
	5		
	10		
	15		
Cooling	20		
	25		
	30		

Temperature Graph

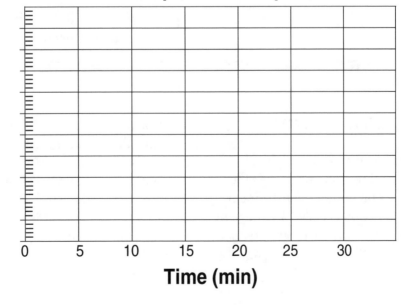

Temperature ( )

Time (min)

FREE AS THE WIND

PRIMARY CONTENT
- Measuring and recording wind direction
- Understanding variability in wind direction

PRIOR STUDENT KNOWLEDGE
Understanding the basic concept of air pressure and understanding that air moves from areas of relatively higher pressure toward areas of lower pressure

PRE-ACTIVITY PREPARATION
1. Obtain standard-length (19.7 cm [$7\frac{3}{4}$ in.]) plastic straws without the flexible segments that allow the straws to bend. Prepare a straw for each group as directed in Teacher Information.
2. Obtain for each group one small bead with a hole diameter large enough to allow the insertion of a straight pin.
3. Copy reproducible Wind Vane Patterns and Data Table (page 39) for each group.
4. Plan this activity on a day when moderate-to-strong winds are forecast.

PROCESS SKILLS
Observing, comparing, inferring, measuring, recording data, identifying variables, experimenting

GROUP SIZE
2–3 students

MATERIALS PER GROUP
- Reproducible Wind Vane Patterns and Data Table
- Scissors
- Several rolls of transparent tape (for whole class)
- 1 index card, 3 in. x 5 in.
- Crayons
- 1 prepared plastic straw
- 1 stapler (for teacher use)
- 1 straight pin (for teacher use)
- 1 small bead as described in Pre-Activity Preparation
- 1 unsharpened pencil with an unused eraser
- 1 electric fan (for teacher use)
- (Optional) magnetic compass (for teacher use)

TEACHER INFORMATION

Wind is the transfer or movement of air. Wind consists of two elements: direction and speed. This activity treats wind direction only. The instrument used to measure wind direction is called a wind vane or weather vane, the arrow of which always points to the direction *from which* the wind is blowing.

Accordingly, winds are always named for or described by the direction from which they come. For example, a north wind blows from north toward south, while a southerly wind moves from the south toward the north. While the wind vane constructed by students in this activity responds well to most winds, friction at the axis (straight pin) may make it less sensitive to light breezes.

To prepare a standard-length straw for this activity, use scissors or a single-edge razor blade to cut a slit at each end of the straw. Make one slit 4 cm ($1\frac{9}{16}$ in.) long and make the other slit 1.5 cm ($\frac{9}{16}$ in.) long. Also make a hole in the straw at a point 7.6 cm (3 in.) from the end that has the longer slit. Use a sewing needle with a diameter a little larger than that of the straight pin to make the hole (so that the straw can swivel easily around the straight pin). Make sure that the hole and both slits are made in the same plane (see illustration immediately following Procedure step 8). For quick straw preparation without measurements, the reproducible Wind Vane Patterns and Data Table includes a pattern against which you can lay a straw—the slit lengths and hole position for a standard straw are indicated, and you can mark them on the straw with a felt-tip pen.

PROCEDURE

1. Review with students the fact that wind is the response of air to differences in air pressure, with wind blowing from areas of relatively higher pressure toward areas of lower pressure.

2. Ask students if they know how meteorologists (scientists who study the weather) measure wind directions. Indicate that they use an instrument called a wind vane (or weather vane) for such measurements. Today, students will make their own wind vanes and use them to measure actual wind directions.

3. A knowledge of compass directions is vital for measuring wind. Introduce students to directions based on an eight-point compass (see illustration).

4. Take the class outside and, using easily recognizable reference points, familiarize students with the eight basic directions. (Optional) You may use a magnetic compass to establish the directions. Move the class to different parts of the school grounds and practice using the reference points to determine directions from several locations.

5. Return to the classroom and divide the class into groups. Distribute to each group all the materials except the straight pins.

6. Instruct groups to detach the Wind Direction Data Table from the reproducible by cutting on the dashed lines. They should set the table aside for later use. Then have them detach the arrow/tail section by cutting on the dashed lines. They should tape that section to a 3 in. x 5 in. index card and then follow the taped pattern to cut out the arrow and the tail separately from the index card.

7. Allow groups to color both sides of the cardboard arrow and tail however they wish.

8. An illustration of the prepared straw is shown below. Instruct students to slip the tail into the longer slit and the arrow into the shorter slit.

(continues)

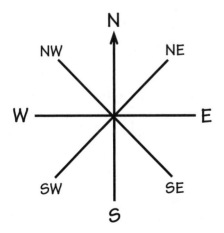

9. Circulate among the groups with a stapler. With each straw, be sure the tail and arrow are both fully inserted and centered in the slits. Using a single staple for each, attach the tail and the arrow to the straw. Try to position the ends of both staples as close to the ends of the straw as possible (see the illustration following Procedure step 10).

10. For each straw, insert a straight pin through the prepared hole and then through the small bead. Assist groups with attaching the wind vane arrow to its shaft (pencil) by vertically inserting the pin into the pencil eraser. The head of the pin should extend a little above the straw so that it will not interfere with the free movement of the straw. The completed wind vane is shown in the illustration.

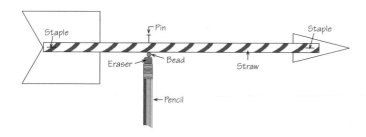

11. Turn a fan onto medium or high speed. Ask one group to come forward with their completed vane. Instruct one student to hold the vane and stand in front of the fan. The student should hold the vane in a vertical position directly in the air flow.

12. Have the class observe whether the arrow of the vane points in the direction from which the wind is coming or in the direction to which the wind is going. Note: if a vane is not contained completely within the air flow (if air on one side of the vane is moving faster than air on the other side), the vane will likely rotate continuously instead of pointing.

13. Repeat steps 11 and 12 with as many groups as you wish. Be sure all students realize that a wind vane will always point in the direction from which the wind is coming. Then discuss with the class how winds are named (see Teacher Information).

14. Assign each group a specific location on the school grounds at which they will measure wind directions. Vary the locations as much as possible (at various spots out in the open, near different sides of the building, near trees, under trees, and so on).

15. Each group is to measure the wind direction at their assigned location three times during the day (mid-morning recess, lunch time, and mid-afternoon recess, for example) and record results on their Wind Direction Data Tables.

16. Following the afternoon measurement, review the results with the class. Most likely, the results will show the following. At any given location, directions will probably not be the same for all three readings. At any given time, directions will probably not be the same at all measuring sites. At any given time, directions will be most consistent for measurements taken out in the open and most variable for measurements taken near buildings, trees, or other structures. Be aware, however, that almost any set of results is possible with winds.

17. Discuss the fact that general wind direction is controlled by the positions of high and low pressure systems, with winds blowing from high pressure toward lower pressure. As these systems move during the day, wind directions change. Structures (buildings and trees, for example) interfere with wind flow and create eddies and currents in all directions. Consequently, the best wind readings are those taken out in the open.

EXTENSIONS AND ADAPTATIONS

1. Have the class measure wind direction from one specific site on the school grounds on a regular basis. Keep a record of measurements on the chalkboard or on a poster board chart.

2. Have students listen to the weather on TV or radio and record the wind direction reported. Students can maintain individual logs and/or a class log of data.

3. Discuss with students various ways wind is (or was) used to do work. (for example: sailing ships, wind surfing, hot air balloons; windmills to grind grain, pump water, and produce electricity)

FREE AS THE WIND

WIND VANE PATTERNS AND DATA TABLE

Name

←——— Slit ———→   Hole   ←Slit→

WIND DIRECTION DATA TABLE

GROUP MEMBERS:

SITE LOCATION:

Observation Time	Wind Direction

TO EVAP OR NOT TO EVAP

PRIMARY CONTENT

Understanding amount of evaporation as a function of the surface area of the water

PRIOR STUDENT KNOWLEDGE

The concept of evaporation

PRE-ACTIVITY PREPARATION

Copy reproducible Student Data Sheet (page 43), one copy per student.

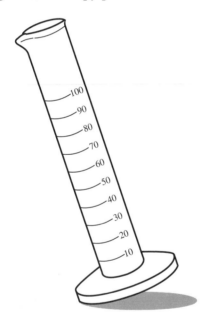

PROCESS SKILLS

Observing, comparing, inferring, measuring, recording data, communicating, hypothesizing, identifying variables, experimenting

GROUP SIZE

2–4 students

MATERIALS PER GROUP

- Masking tape
- 1 straight-sided container with a narrow opening (olive jar or 177 mL [6 oz] juice can, for example) (small container opening)
- 1 large aluminum pie pan (large container opening)
- 1 small aluminum pot-pie pan or plastic cereal bowl (medium container opening)
- 1 pencil
- 1 sheet of paper
- Available water (for whole class)
- 1 graduated cylinder or other type of measuring container
- 1 copy of reproducible Student Data Sheet for each student
- 1 ruler for each student
- Crayons or colored pencils for each student

TEACHER INFORMATION

Evaporation of water occurs at the water-air interface or, in other words, at the surface of the water. It is here that movement of water molecules causes them to leave their liquid surrounding and move into the air. Evaporation does not occur below the water surface. Consequently, with a given amount of water, the more water that is exposed to the air (the greater the surface area), the greater the amount of evaporation.

PROCEDURE

1. If necessary, review with the class the general concept of evaporation. Then ask students to name as many things (variables) as they can that would influence how much water will evaporate in a given amount of time. *(Depending on previous work with evaporation, students will frequently give the response of air temperature and wind movement; they may occasionally mention relative humidity, but they will rarely mention the amount of surface area of the water.)*

2. Inform students that in today's activity they will be investigating how the amount of surface area of water affects the amount of evaporation. Define surface area for students and discuss as necessary.

3. Group students and distribute all the materials except the rulers and crayons. Direct each group to use strips of masking tape to label the 3 containers with the names or initials of the group members.

4. Briefly outline the activity procedure (steps 5–9) and then instruct students in each group to develop and record on a piece of paper a prediction regarding the effect of surface area on evaporation, including an explanation as to why they made that prediction.

5. Have groups test their predictions by putting the same amount of water into each of the 3 containers. For a given group, the amount of water does not matter as long as it is exactly the same for each container. The amount must be great enough, however, to completely cover the bottom of the large pie pan, yet small enough to be held within the smallest container. Each student should record this starting amount of water for each of the three containers in the Data Table on the Student Data Sheet.

6. Each group should carefully move its containers to a location in the classroom where they can remain undisturbed for one to three days.

7. After at least half the water has evaporated from the large pie pans (one to five days depending on room conditions and starting amounts), have each group retrieve all 3 containers.

8. Groups are to carefully measure the amount of water remaining in each container by pouring the water back into the measuring container. Caution students to be extra careful not to spill any water! Each student should record on the Data Table the final amount of water in each container. Each student should then calculate the total amount of water that evaporated from each container and record each of those amounts on the Data Table.

9. Distribute rulers and crayons. Direct each student to display the evaporation amounts as a bar graph. Because of variation in starting amounts and units of measure, values and units are not provided for the vertical axis on the graph on the Student Data Sheet. Assist students, therefore, with the labeling of this axis.

10. Conduct a session to review and discuss results. Include questions such as:

    - At the beginning of the experiment, was there the same amount of water in each of the 3 containers? *(yes)* What was this amount? *(Answers will vary.)*

    - Were all 3 containers subject to the same room conditions (temperature and air movement, for example)? *(yes)*

    - What was the only difference among the containers that would affect evaporation? *(the size of the container opening, which controlled the surface area of water exposed to the air)*

    - Which container—which amount of surface area—showed the most evaporation? The least evaporation? *(Water in the large pie pan had the greatest surface area and displayed the most evaporation. Water in the container with the smallest opening had the least surface area and displayed the least amount of evaporation.)*

    - How much water evaporated from each of the 3 containers. *(Answers will vary.)*

    - Was your prediction correct? *(Answers will vary.)*

    - What is the relationship between surface area and the amount of evaporation? *(Other factors being equal, as the surface area increases, so does the amount of evaporation.)*

    - Why do you think this is the case? (See Teacher Information and discuss the explanation with the class.)

(continues)

(continued)

11. It is likely that the amount of water evaporated from a given size container will vary slightly among the groups. Ask students if they can think of reasons (variables) to explain this variation. In this activity, such variation is most likely due to inexact measurements, errors in measurement, water spillage, and rounding of measurements.

EXTENSIONS AND ADAPTATIONS

1. This activity is appropriate for use in a learning center.

2. Use additional containers to add to the sequence of surface area amounts.

3. Related activity Disappearing Water on page 44.

TO EVAP OR NOT TO EVAP _____

STUDENT DATA SHEET

Name_____

DATA TABLE

Water Surface Area (size of container opening)	Starting Amount of Water	Final Amount of Water	Total Amount of Water Evaporated
Small			
Medium			
Large			

BAR GRAPH

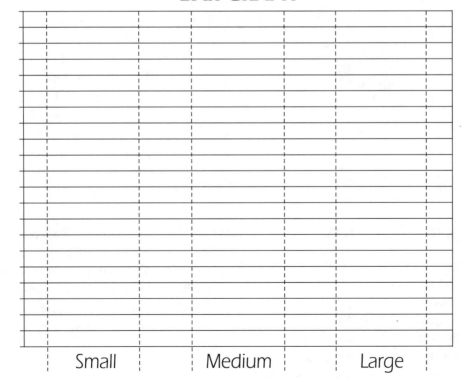

Water Surface Area (size of container opening)

DISAPPEARING WATER

PRIMARY CONTENT
- Evaporation as a function of the relative humidity of air
- The concepts of moisture capacity and saturation

PRIOR STUDENT KNOWLEDGE
The concept of evaporation

PRE-ACTIVITY PREPARATION
Copy reproducible Student Data Sheet (page 47), one copy per student.

PROCESS SKILLS
Observing, comparing, inferring, measuring, recording data, communicating, hypothesizing, identifying variables, experimenting

GROUP SIZE
2–4 students

MATERIALS PER GROUP
- Masking tape
- 3 clear plastic cups, 177 mL–355 mL (6 oz–12 oz), all the same size
- 1 sheet of paper
- 1 pencil
- 1 graduated cylinder or other measuring container
- Available water (for whole class)
- 1 copy of reproducible Student Data Sheet for each student
- 2 sections of aluminum foil, roughly 10 cm x 10 cm (4 in. x 4 in.)
- 2 rubber bands of a size that fits snugly around the top of the plastic cups
- 1 ruler for each student
- Crayons or colored pencils for each student

TEACHER INFORMATION

Air has a limit or capacity as to the amount of water vapor it can hold. This limit is called the moisture capacity, and it varies directly with temperature. Air molecules at a given temperature have only a certain amount of free space between them that can be occupied by water vapor molecules. How full air is of water vapor—the proportion of free space (moisture capacity) being occupied by water vapor molecules— is referred to as the relative humidity. Air that is completely full of water vapor has a relative humidity of 100% and is said to be saturated; air that is holding only half of it capacity of water vapor molecules (air that is half full) has a relative humidity of 50%, and so on.

Relative humidity is a major factor determining the amount and rate of evaporation since it, in essence, represents the number of available openings for new water vapor molecules. The higher the relative humidity of air, the less and the slower the evaporation, and vice versa. There will be no evaporation at all into air that is saturated. A good analogy is that of a group of people waiting to take an elevator. The fewer the number of people in the elevator when it arrives, the more space there is available for new passengers and so the greater the number of people waiting who can get on. The fuller the elevator is when it arrives, the less space there is available for new passengers, and the fewer the number of people who can get on.

In this activity, the small amount of air in the cup with the cover lacking holes quickly becomes saturated. Since that air has no access to drier room air, it cannot mix with the drier air and reduce its relative humidity. Consequently, it stays saturated and no more evaporation occurs. In fact, the tiny amount of evaporation that it took to bring the air in the cup up to saturation will not even be measurable. The air in the cup with the cover having holes has limited access to drier room air. Thus some mixing with room air will occur, allowing a reduction in relative humidity, resulting in some continuous evaporation. The air in the uncovered cup has free access to drier room air. Maximum mixing will occur, causing the air in that cup to have the lowest relative humidity. As a result, maximum evaporation will take place from that cup.

PROCEDURE

1. If necessary, review with the class the general concept of evaporation. Then ask students if they think air has a limit, or capacity, with regard to how much water vapor it can hold—that is, can evaporation proceed indefinitely into a given volume of air, or can air get full of water vapor, causing evaporation to stop? Let students express their ideas but do not provide answers or content information at this time.

2. Tell students that today they will begin an experiment to find the answer to that question.

3. Group students and distribute all the materials except the rulers and crayons. Ask each group to use strips of masking tape to label the 3 cups with the names or initials of group members.

4. Briefly outline the activity procedure (steps 5–12). Then instruct students in each group to develop and record on a piece of paper a prediction regarding the relationship between the amount of evaporation and the access of cup air to room air, including an explanation as to why they made that prediction.

5. Have each group test their prediction by using the measuring container to put the same amount of water into each of their 3 cups. They should fill each cup roughly halfway; for a given group, however, the exact amount of water does not matter as long as it is the same for each cup. Each student should record this starting amount of water for each cup in the Data Table on the Student Data Sheet.

6. Have each group leave one cup uncovered, the water in this cup having access to the air in the cup which, in turn, has free access to the air in the room.

7. Ask each group to cover the opening of a second cup with foil, folding the excess foil down around the cup and securing it tightly with a rubber band or masking tape. Students should use a pencil to poke 4 or 5 holes through the foil covering. The water in this cup has access to the air in the cup which, in turn, has limited access to the air in the room.

(continues)

(continued)

8. Students should cover the opening of the third cup with foil, folding the excess foil down around the cup and securing it tightly with a rubber band or masking tape. They should not poke holes in this covering. The water in this cup has access only to the air inside the cup.

9. Groups should move their cups to a location in the room where the cups can remain undisturbed.

10. After about one-half to three-fourths of the water has evaporated from the open containers (one to three days, depending on room conditions and starting amounts), have groups retrieve all their cups.

11. Each group is to carefully measure the amount of water remaining in each cup by pouring the water back into the measuring container. Caution students to be extra careful not to spill any water! Each student should record on the Data Table the final amount of water for each cup. Each student should then calculate and record on the Data Table the total amount of water that evaporated from each cup.

12. Distribute rulers and crayons. Direct each student to display the evaporation amounts as a bar graph. Because of variation in starting amounts and units of measure, values and units are not provided for the vertical axis on the graph on the Student Data Sheet. Assist students, therefore, with the labeling of this axis.

13. Conduct a session to review and discuss results. Include questions such as:

    • At the beginning of the experiment, was there the same amount of water in each of the 3 cups? *(yes)* What was this amount? *(Answers will vary.)*

    • Were all 3 cups subject to the same room conditions (temperature and air movement, for example)? *(yes)*

    • What was the only difference among the cups that would affect evaporation? *(access of the air in the cups to the air in the room, ranging from no access to free access)*

    • In which cup was there the most evaporation? The least evaporation? *(Evaporation was greatest from the cup with no covering [free access to room air]. The least evaporation occurred from the cup with the covering lacking holes [no access to room air].)*

    • How much water evaporated from each of the 3 cups? *(Answers will vary.)*

    • Was your prediction correct? *(Answers will vary.)*

    • How might you explain these results? *(Answers will vary.)*

14. Use the last question as the basis for a discussion and explanation of evaporation as a function of how full air is of water vapor. Introduce the terms *relative humidity, moisture capacity,* and *saturation* (see Teacher Information).

15. It is likely that the amount of water evaporated from a given type of cup will vary slightly among groups. Ask students if they can think of reasons (variables) to explain this variation. *(Examples include inexact measurements, errors in measurement, water spillage, rounding of measurements, differences in the number and/or sizes of holes in the foil covering, and differences in the tightness of the seal between the coverings and the cups.)*

EXTENSIONS AND ADAPTATIONS

1. This activity is appropriate for use in a learning center.

2. Ask students to identify environments that tend to stay damp as a result of high relative humidity inhibiting evaporation. *(Examples include basements and cellars, locker rooms, and indoor swimming pool areas.)*

3. Related activity To Evap or Not to Evap on page 40.

DISAPPEARING WATER

STUDENT DATA SHEET

Name_____

DATA TABLE

Access to Drier Room Air	Starting Amount of Water	Final Amount of Water	Total Amount of Water Evaporated
None (cup and cover with no holes)			
Limited (cup and cover with holes)			
Free (cup without a cover)			

BAR GRAPH

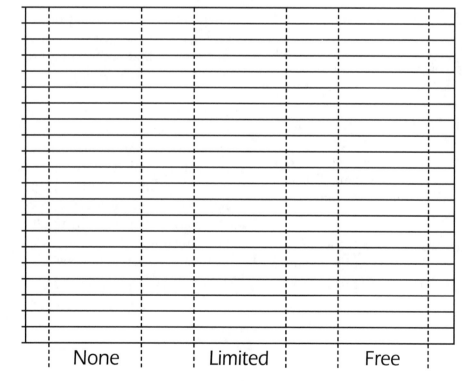

Amount of Water Evaporated

None   Limited   Free

Access to Drier Air

RAINBOW BRITE _____

PRIMARY CONTENT

Rainbows and rainbow formation

PRIOR STUDENT KNOWLEDGE

No special prior knowledge is required.

PRE-ACTIVITY PREPARATION

1. Collect several color pictures of rainbows from magazines or other sources to show to the class.
2. You need to do this activity on a bright, sunny day.

PROCESS SKILLS

Observing, inferring, communicating

GROUP SIZE

Whole class and individual

MATERIALS PER GROUP

*   1 dishpan or similar container (for teacher demonstration)
*   1 hand mirror (for teacher demonstration)
*   Available water (for teacher demonstration)
*   Crayons or colored pencils for each student
*   Several sheets of plain white paper for each student

TEACHER INFORMATION

Sunlight is white light because it is composed of light (wavelengths of energy) of all the primary colors. When white light is passed through a prism, it is separated into its component colors: red, orange, yellow, green, blue, indigo, and violet (thus the mnemonic ROY G. BIV), with red representing the longest wavelengths and violet the shortest wavelengths. Because some colors (indigo, for example) are more difficult to see than others in rainbows or prism spectrums, students are often unable to distinctly observe all seven colors.

Small droplets of water suspended in the air after a rain act like tiny prisms, breaking white sunlight down into its primary colors, resulting in a rainbow.

Rainbows, composed only of light and typically taking a broad arched shape, are common sky phenomena that occur when a rain is immediately followed by bright, sunny conditions. (Note: there are also requirements regarding the angle of the sun relative to the horizon and the sun's position relative to the observer; these requirements, however, are somewhat technical, especially for elementary students.) In this activity, water overlying a mirror acts as a rudimentary prism, separating the sunlight reflected off the mirror into its component wavelengths (colors). The result is a rainbow-like phenomenon, although not as well-developed or distinct as an actual rainbow.

PROCEDURE

1. Introduce the activity by asking students questions such as those that follow. Listen to responses but do not present information or make corrections at this time.

   - How many of you have ever seen a rainbow?

   - Where should a person look to see a rainbow?

   - When do rainbows occur?

   - Is it always sunny or cloudy when rainbows are seen?

   - What shape are rainbows?

   - What are rainbows made of? Are they solid?

   - What colors do you see in rainbows?

2. Show students pictures of rainbows and ask them to identify the colors they see (see Teacher Information). Then ask the students if they think a rainbow could be created right here in the classroom.

3. In the classroom, next to a window through which bright, direct sunlight is shining, place a dishpan with 8 cm–15 cm (3 in.–6 in.) of water.

4. As much as possible, eliminate all sources of light in the classroom with the exception of the single lighted window.

5. Place the mirror on the bottom of the pan (underwater) and position it so that it is receiving full, direct sunlight.

6. Keeping the mirror underwater, tilt it until a rainbow is visible on the ceiling or wall. Ask students to identify the colors and the color sequence visible in the rainbow.

7. As students continue to observe the rainbow, discuss with them the basic concepts associated with rainbows (see Teacher Information), especially as they relate to the questions in step 1. If you wish, you can repeat those questions following the discussion.

8. End the demonstration and return the room to normal lighting.

9. Distribute crayons and plain paper to students. Have students each write a creative, make-believe story which centers in some way around a rainbow. Ask students to create pictures (especially rainbows) to illustrate their stories.

10. Let students read their stories to the class.

EXTENSIONS AND ADAPTATIONS

1. This activity is appropriate for use in a learning center.

2. Try the activity with different water depths, different mirror sizes, and/or different lighting conditions.

3. Have the class conduct a Rainbow Watch in which students report their observations of real rainbows.

4. Suggest to students that on a bright, sunny day at home they should spray water from a garden hose so that it exits the nozzle in a fine spray or mist. If they stand with the sun behind them, students will see a nice rainbow within the mist where sunlight is passing through.

5. Hold a prism in the window so that it is exposed to bright sunlight. Adjust its position until a spectrum (rainbow) is produced. Depending on several factors, it is possible that you can project the spectrum onto the ceiling or wall. If this does not work, have a student hold a white sheet of paper in front of the prism at varying distances and angles until the spectrum is displayed. Also try shining a flashlight beam through a prism in a dark room.

6. Under bright, sunlit conditions, place water in a shallow, flat pan. Add several drops of motor oil to the water. Have students observe as multicolored swirls form in the water.

7. Have Roy G. Biv week (see Teacher Information). On each day, have students wear a specific color of the rainbow.

ON CLOUD NINE _____

PRIMARY CONTENT
- The concept of condensation
- The concepts of fog (cloud) formation and dew formation

PRIOR STUDENT KNOWLEDGE

Understanding the concepts of evaporation and saturation; suggested completion of the activity Disappearing Water on page 44

PRE-ACTIVITY PREPARATION

No pre-activity preparation is required.

PROCESS SKILLS

Observing, inferring

GROUP SIZE

2–5 students, followed by whole class

MATERIALS PER GROUP
- 1 metal can (soup can) with label removed (for each group)
- 1 plastic cup or other container for scooping and transporting ice (for each group)
- 1 cooler of ice (for whole class)
- Available water (for whole class)
- 1 sink or disposal bucket (for whole class)
- Desk top (for each group)
- 1 hot plate (for teacher demonstration)
- 1 teakettle (for teacher demonstration)
- 1 large strainer (for teacher demonstration)

TEACHER INFORMATION

When air is cooled, the air molecules lose energy and move closer together, reducing the space available for water molecules (cold air has a lesser moisture capacity than does warmer air). Consequently, if air is cooled enough and if the air temperature is above freezing, water vapor will be released from the air as tiny liquid droplets. This process is known as condensation. If the temperature is below freezing, the vapor will be released as tiny ice crystals, a process known as deposition.

This activity demonstrates condensation in air that is cooled in two different ways: through contact with a cold surface (conductional cooling) and through mixing with colder surrounding air. The former occurs in step 9 (which models the formation of dew via condensation on the surface of a cold can) and in step 14 (which models the formation of fog via condensation in the atmosphere). The latter occurs in step 12 which also models a method of fog creation via atmospheric condensation.

Fog and clouds are alike in most respects—they are very similar in appearance and composition, and both require the cooling of air with resultant condensation (or deposition) in the atmosphere. For students at the 2–3 level, it is suggested that you highlight only one difference between the two—the fact that fog occurs at the surface, while clouds occur in the upper atmosphere. In actuality, there is another difference. Clouds form only through a more complex process called adiabatic cooling (cooling due to volume expansion of air); fog is created by conductional cooling against the colder earth's surface and sometimes by cooling due to mixing of air. It is recommended that you reserve the treatment of adiabatic cooling for a higher level.

PROCEDURE

1. Introduce the activity by taking the class outside to observe the clouds. Ask students if they see any shapes made by the clouds (people, figures, animals, for example). Then let students take turns relating those shapes to the class. Also ask students to imagine that they are up in the clouds and ask them to tell you how it feels and what they see.

2. Return to the classroom. (Optional)—Have students do a creative writing assignment about what it is like up in the clouds. Let students read their descriptions to the class.

3. Prime the class with questions such as those that follow. Listen to responses but do not provide answers or content information at this time.
   - What is a cloud?
   - Can you stand on one?
   - How do you think clouds are formed?
   - What is fog?
   - Have you ever gone walking in a fog? If so, describe your experience.
   - How are clouds and fog different? The same?

4. If necessary, review with the class the general concept of evaporation, including the fact that, other factors being equal, more evaporation will occur into air that is warm than into air that is cold. Remind students that this is due to greater molecular spacing between the faster-moving molecules of warm air, thus providing more available space for water molecules.

5. Ask students, "If liquid water can change and go into the air as a gas (evaporation), do you think the reverse can happen—can water vapor change and come back out of the air as a liquid?" Let students discuss this possibility and then tell them that today's activity will provide the answer.

6. Group students and distribute a metal can and plastic carrying cup to each group. Also point out the ice, water, and disposal bucket. Provide groups with instructions and questions as delineated in steps 7–9.

7. Have students in each group rub their fingers on the outside of the can. Ask, "Is it completely dry?" *(yes)* Now have them fill the can to about three-fourths with lukewarm water—not cold! (Note: you may wish to adjust the temperature of the water coming from the tap yourself to insure that it is tepid.) Caution students to be careful not to get any water on the outside of the can.

8. Ask students in each group to set the can on a desk and observe it for a minute or two, touching the outside of the can in the process. Ask questions such as those that follow.
   - Was the outside of the can dry before water was added? *(yes)*
   - Is the outside of the can still dry? *(yes)*
   - Does this show that the can is not leaking any water? *(yes)*

9. Now each group is to empty the water from the can into the sink or disposal bucket. Then using the plastic cup, students should retrieve ice from the cooler and completely fill the can. Caution students to be careful not to get any ice on the outside of the can. Have students observe the can for several minutes, touching its outside in the process. Ask questions such as those that follow.
   - Is the outside of the can still dry? *(No; students should both see and feel liquid water on the outside of the ice filled can.)*
   - Did this water on the outside of the can leak out of the can? *(no, as was previously established)*
   - How does the temperature of the outside of the ice-filled can compare to that of the water-filled can? *(The outside of the ice-filled can is much colder.)*
   - What do you think that cold surface does to the air right next to the can—air that is actually touching the can? *(It makes that air colder.)*
   - Can cold air hold as much water vapor as warmer air? *(no)*
   - Then where do you think the water on the outside of the cold can came from? (Explain as necessary. *The water came from the air. When the air was chilled, it could not hold as much water vapor as when it was warm. Thus water vapor was released by the air in the form of liquid water on the side of the can.*)

(continues)

(continued)

10. Introduce the term *condensation* for the process that students just observed. Relate that process to the formation of dew during the night when air in contact with a colder earth's surface is chilled.

11. Now have all students gather around you to see a demonstration of fog (cloud) formation.

12. Boil water in the teakettle until steam comes out of the spout. (You might wish to have the teakettle already heating to save time.) Tell students that what they are seeing is a tiny model of fog or a cloud.

13. Ask students if they can explain why the fog/cloud is forming and why it disappears some distance above the spout. *(The warm, saturated air coming out of the spout is cooled by mixing with the cooler room air. As with the ice-filled can, this cooling results in condensation and the formation of tiny droplets—the fog/cloud forms. The droplets then evaporate back into the drier air, causing the fog or cloud to disappear.)*

14. Cause the fog/cloud to reform by filling the strainer with ice and positioning it a few inches above the point where the steam is disappearing—a position that allows the warm, high-humidity air from the kettle to continue to rise up through the strainer (see illustration). Students should easily observe a distinct cloud form around and above the strainer.

15. Use questions such as those that follow to discuss with students the reoccurrence of the cloud.

    • What caused the cloud to reform? *(high-humidity air being cooled by contact with the ice, resulting in condensation)*

    • What, then, is a cloud or fog composed of? *(tiny water droplets)*

    • Can a person stand or walk on clouds? *(No, clouds are not solid.)*

16. Discuss how the cooling of air is also necessary for fog and cloud formation in nature. Discuss how fog and clouds are alike and how they are different (see Teacher Information).

EXTENSIONS AND ADAPTATIONS

Pour about 2.5 cm (1 in.) of warm water into a tall, clear wide-mouth container (a quart canning jar or a 2 L plastic soda bottle with the upper portion cut off, for example). Hold a burning match down inside the container for a few seconds then drop the match. Immediately cover the top of the container with aluminum foil. Wait a minute or two and then set several ice cubes on top of the foil. A dim cloud should become apparent in the container. It will become even more visible if you darken the room and shine a flashlight through the container. With close observation, students can even see tiny droplets of water swirling in the air of the container.

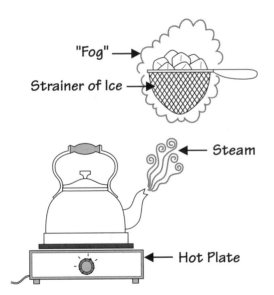

"Fog" →

Strainer of Ice →

← Steam

← Hot Plate

RAINY GAUGE

PRIMARY CONTENT

- Constructing a rain gauge
- Measuring, recording, and graphing rainfall amounts
- Analyzing precipitation data

PRIOR STUDENT KNOWLEDGE

Experience with graphing

PRE-ACTIVITY PREPARATION

1. Each student will need a clean clear jar with straight sides and a flat bottom. From the standpoint of safety, it is preferable that you use plastic jars (some sizes and brands of peanut butter come in plastic jars with straight sides). Ask students to bring jars from home. You will need one extra jar for a gauge-construction demonstration.

2. Copy reproducibles Daily Precipitation Chart (page 56) and Daily Precipitation Graph (page 57) for each student.

PROCESS SKILLS

Observing, comparing, inferring, measuring, recording data, communicating, identifying variables

GROUP SIZE

Individual

MATERIALS PER GROUP

- 1 clear plastic jar with straight sides and a flat bottom
- 1 ruler
- 1 black permanent marker
- 1 clear jar to use in a gauge-construction demonstration (for whole class)
- 1 copy of reproducible Daily Precipitation Chart
- 1 copy of reproducible and Daily Precipitation Graph

TEACHER INFORMATION

A rain gauge is a simple instrument used to measure precipitation. In the United States, precipitation is usually measured in inches; in most other countries, metric measurement is used. The rain gauge is simply an open calibrated container which catches precipitation as it falls. A properly located gauge should be in an open area away from overhanging trees.

Precipitation is normally reported for a twenty-four-hour period. At the end of that period (midnight for official readings), the gauge is checked. If it is dry, zero precipitation is recorded for the period. If it contains water, the amount is recorded and the gauge is emptied for the next twenty-four-hour period. Precipitation is always given in water equivalent. Thus, precipitation in the solid form must be melted to obtain a reading. For this reason, it is strongly suggested that you conduct this activity during a warm month when rain is the typical precipitation.

(continues)

(continued)

Precipitation amounts usually show significant variation even within a fairly restricted area (a county, a town, or even a smaller area). There are a variety of reasons for this variation, such as: (a) precipitation does not form equally (in the same amount) throughout the extent of a cloud and will therefore not fall in equal amounts on areas beneath that cloud; (b) winds within a storm system blow and scatter falling precipitation in diverse patterns; and (c) topography or man-made obstructions (tall buildings, for example), combined with blowing precipitation, may cause some areas to be more sheltered than others.

A missed reading is no problem if no precipitation has occurred since the last reading. In this case, the amount in the gauge is the amount that occurred during the previous period. The gauge can be emptied, the reading recorded for the previous period, and observations can continue as normal. If precipitation has occurred since the missed reading, there can be no correction or substitution due to the spatial variability in precipitation amounts. In this case, no data should be recorded or graphed for the overlapping periods. The gauge should be emptied at the next measurement time, with observations beginning again.

PROCEDURE

1. Introduce the activity by asking students questions such as those that follow, presenting explanations as necessary:

   - What does the term *precipitation* mean? *(Precipitation is any form of water [rain, snow, sleet, or hail] falling from clouds and reaching the surface.)*

   - What instrument is used to measure the amount of precipitation? *(rain gauge)*

   - If we wanted to compare precipitation amounts measured on thirty different days, how could we remember what the amounts were each of those days? *(The data would have to be recorded; recording data assists the recall and organization of the data.)*

   - Should we measure the precipitation amount at the same location each day? Why? *(yes, because of the spatial variability in precipitation amounts; see Teacher Information)*

2. Discuss with the class the operating principle of a rain gauge (see Teacher Information).

3. Tell students that they are going to be meteorologists for the next month—taking, recording, and examining precipitation amounts on a daily basis at each of their homes. To accomplish this task, they will each need to construct a rain gauge.

4. Using the extra jar, a ruler, and a permanent marker, demonstrate for the class how to make a rain gauge. The scale may be in inches (marked at every quarter inch) or centimeters (marked at every half centimeter). The accompanying illustration shows a gauge in inches. (Note: whatever scale you select, make sure that all of the students' rain gauges use the same scale.)

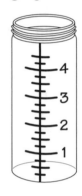

5. Distribute to each student all the materials except the reproducibles and have them each construct a rain gauge.

6. Inform students that they will be measuring precipitation amounts at their homes for a period of one month using their own rain gauges. Each gauge should be placed in as open an area as possible where it will not be disturbed. For consistency, all gauges should be read to the nearest quarter inch (or nearest half centimeter). If there is rain in the gauge, but it is not enough to be measured (closer to zero than to the quarter-inch or half-centimeter mark), students should record the amount as Trace.

7. Also indicate that students should read and empty the gauges at the same time each day, or as close as possible to that time. Decide on the best time for the majority of the class. If you select 7:00 A.M., for example, then each reading would represent the total precipitation for the twenty-four-hour period of 7:00 A.M. one day to 7:00 A.M. the next day. Tell students to read and empty their gauges at the assigned time even if it is raining at that time.

8. Give each student a Daily Precipitation Chart to keep at home for recording precipitation amounts. Students should write the days of the month numerically in the small boxes in the upper-left corners. Assist students with this task as necessary.

9. Students should read each measurement, including any zeros (no precipitation), in the larger space on the chart for the day that the reading is taken. Encourage students to record their readings as soon as the gauge is emptied and reset—not to wait until later in the day! Also include an explanation as to how they should handle missing data (see Teacher Information).

10. At the end of the month, students should bring their precipitation data to class. Assist them as necessary with reading and completing the other information asked for on the chart.

11. Distribute a Daily Precipitation Graph to each student. Because of the choice of units of measure, units are not provided for the vertical axis on the graph. Assist students with the labeling of this axis. Have each student plot his/her home data as a bar graph. Ask students to explain the advantage of graphing the information. *(Graphs aid in the interpretation of data because trends and changes become visually apparent; graphs also allow for easy visual comparisons of two or more sets of data.)*

12. Have students compare their graphs. Conduct a discussion of results, including questions such as:

    - How do the daily precipitation amounts compare? *(In all probability, daily results will vary considerably.)*

    - What was the total amount of precipitation you recorded for the entire month? (Record totals on the board.)

    - How do the monthly precipitation amounts compare? *(Again, there will probably be a significant amount of variation among the monthly totals.)*

    - Is such variation in daily and monthly amounts normal? (see Teacher Information)

    - What do you think is the cause of such variation? (see Teacher Information)

13. Discuss the other information that students completed on the Daily Precipitation Charts (in step 10) as you desire.

EXTENSIONS AND ADAPTATIONS

1. Have students measure and record daily precipitation amounts for several months. This can be home data, or you can set up a gauge at school and have data collected by the class. With students, decide if any observable trends or patterns are present.

2. Using local media forecasts and reports as the source, keep a record of predicted and actual precipitation amounts for a period of time. Let students compare the results and judge the accuracy of the predictions.

3. Obtain monthly precipitation data for various locations in the United States and the world (check a good atlas or a climatology text). Then let students compare precipitation amounts and patterns for those locations with those of their location.

RAINY GAUGE _____

DAILY PRECIPITATION CHART

Name_____

Month _____   **Observation Time** _____

SUNDAY	MONDAY	TUESDAY	WEDNESDAY	THURSDAY	FRIDAY	SATURDAY

Total precipitation for the month: _____

Greatest amount of measured precipitation on one day: _____ on (date) _____

Total number of days with measurable precipitation: _____

Total number of days without measurable precipitation: _____

Longest string of days with measurable precipitation: _____ on

(dates) _____

Longest string of days with no measurable precipitation: _____ on

(dates) _____

RAINY GAUGE _____

DAILY PRECIPITATION GRAPH

Name _____

Month _____

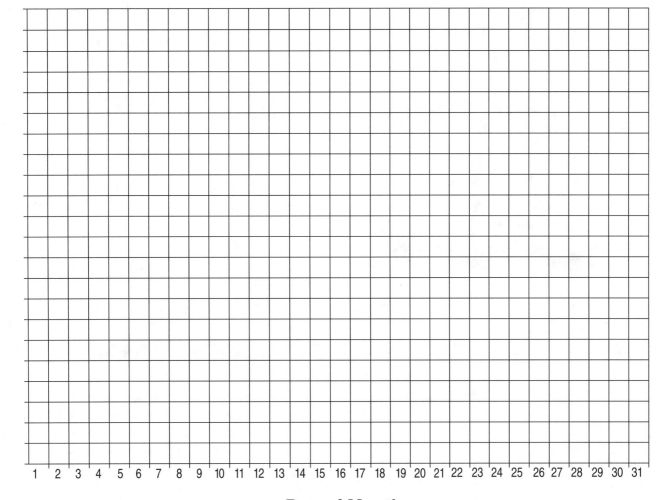

Precipitation Amount ( )

1 2 3 4 5 6 7 8 9 10 11 12 13 14 15 16 17 18 19 20 21 22 23 24 25 26 27 28 29 30 31

Day of Month

AHOY, MATEY

PRIMARY CONTENT
Understanding ocean-drift current circulation

PRIOR STUDENT KNOWLEDGE
The concept of prevailing winds

PRE-ACTIVITY PREPARATION
Copy reproducible Currents and More Currents (page 61), one copy per student.

PROCESS SKILLS
Observing, inferring, predicting, communicating, hypothesizing, experimenting

GROUP SIZE
2–4 students

MATERIALS PER GROUP
- 1 world map (for whole class)
- 1 large, but not necessarily deep, container (baking pan, deep cookie sheet, plastic sweater or shoe box, or aquarium tank, for example); container types can vary from group to group
- Available water (for whole class)
- 1 large plastic cup for transporting water
- 1 punch (1-hole) (for whole class)
- Scrap piece of dark construction paper
- 1 plastic straw for each student
- 1 pencil
- 1 sheet of paper
- 1 blue crayon or blue-colored pencil for each student
- 1 copy of reproducible Currents and More Currents for each student

TEACHER INFORMATION

Drift currents are surface currents caused by the frictional dragging effect of the prevailing winds blowing over the water surface. Most of the large, famous ocean currents, such as the Gulf Stream, are drift currents. The other major type of ocean current is a density current. Density currents are not related to wind, however, but to differences in water density.

In this activity, frictional dragging by wind causes water to move along the left sides of the container (from each blower's reference). Using the procedure

diagram as a reference, students will observe that this movement causes a buildup of water in the upper-left and lower-right corners of the container. Likewise, deficits of water are created in the lower-left and upper-right corners. In response, water flows from the areas of surplus to the areas of deficit. The final result is a complete circulation around the edges of the container in a clockwise direction. This represents drift-current circulation in the Northern Hemisphere. In the Southern Hemisphere, the situation is reversed, and drift-current flow is counterclockwise.

PROCEDURE

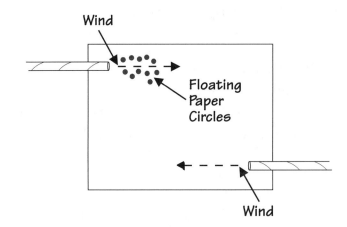

1. If necessary, review with students the fact that prevailing winds are those that blow from one direction more often than from any other direction. Most of the continental United States is located within the prevailing westerly wind belt, where winds blow in a general westerly-to-easterly direction more often than any other.

2. Direct students' attention to the world map. Point out the locations of England and the former American colonies.

3. Inform the class that in the days of colonial America, the sailing ships going from the colonies to England made the trip across the Atlantic Ocean much faster—often two weeks faster—than did ships going from England to the colonies. Ask students if they have any ideas that might explain such a difference in times for equal distances.

4. The most frequently offered suggestion is that ships heading west to America from England had to sail against the prevailing winds. Indicate that this is true and is part of the explanation; however, there is an even more important reason. Tell the class that today's activity will help reveal that reason.

5. Group students and distribute the materials.

6. Instruct each group to fill its large container about three-fourths with water. Students can use the plastic cup for transporting water if necessary. At the same time, one student from each group should punch five to ten holes in the dark construction paper, collecting the little punched-out circles.

7. Groups should put their paper circle particles in the water along one side of the container (see illustration).

8. Within each group, two students are to position themselves one at each end of the container. Students are to blow through the straws, directing the airflow upon the water at a low angle and along the left side of the container (relative to each student). See illustration; the dashed lines show the direction of air flow.

9. Before they begin, have each group develop and record on a plain sheet of paper a prediction regarding the outcome of the experiment, especially with reference to water movement within the container as indicated by movement of the floating paper circles. The prediction may take the form of a sketch illustrating water motion.

10. Now begin the experiment. As the two students blow continuously for a minute or two, other group members are to observe the motion of the water by watching the paper circles. Each observer is to show direction of air flow by drawing arrows with a pencil on the diagram of the setup shown in the upper half of the reproducible. Each is then to record observed water motion by drawing blue arrows on the same diagram.

11. Have the blowers and the observers change places and repeat step 10. If the paper circles are waterlogged, let groups punch out new ones.

12. Now tell each group to experiment with different strengths of airflow (gentle, moderate, and strong). Again, students are to observe the results on water motion.

(continues)

(continued)

13. Conduct a session to discuss results and to present additional information about ocean drift currents as desired (see Teacher Information). Include questions such as:

    • What did the airflow from the straws represent? *(wind—specifically, prevailing wind)*

    • Did the wind cause the water to flow or move? How do you know? *(Yes, the water flowed as was observed by movement of the paper circles.)*

    • How do you know it was the wind moving the water and not just the wind moving the paper? *(because the paper circles lay flat in the water and did not catch any wind)*

    • How does wind move water? *(by dragging the water along with it, due to friction)*

    • Can you describe the pattern of water flow that you observed? *(clockwise around the periphery of the container; see Answer Key on page 154)*

    • How did water motion vary under different wind speeds? *(the stronger the wind, the faster the water flow)*

    • What do we call movement of water such as you created? *(a current)*

    • Would a similar current be formed in the ocean due to the prevailing winds? *(yes)*

14. See if students can transfer what they have learned to an actual situation. Have them complete the lower half of the reproducible by predicting currents in the Atlantic Ocean that form under the prevailing westerly winds and the prevailing (north) easterly winds. Students are to draw in blue arrows showing predicted current directions. (Note: the two wind systems shown on the map have been simplified for students at this level.)

15. Go over actual drift-current circulation in the Atlantic (see Answer Key). Then repeat the question asked in step 3. *(In going to England from the colonies, ships were traveling with the ocean current; the trip from England to the colonies was against the current.)*

EXTENSIONS AND ADAPTATIONS

Related activities 'Round and 'Round She Goes on page 62 and Are You Dense? on page 65.

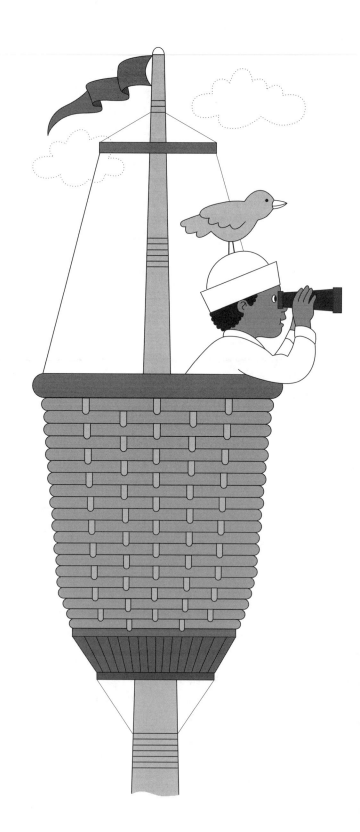

AHOY, MATEY

CURRENTS AND MORE CURRENTS

Name

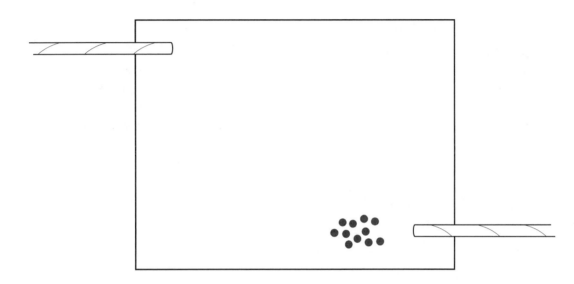

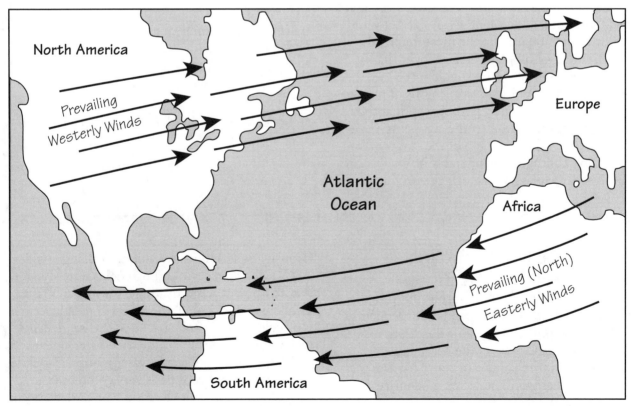

North America

Prevailing
Westerly Winds

Atlantic
Ocean

Europe

Africa

Prevailing (North)

Easterly Winds

South America

'ROUND AND 'ROUND SHE GOES _____

PRIMARY CONTENT

- Understanding the relationship between water temperature and water density
- Understanding convection in water

PRIOR STUDENT KNOWLEDGE

Exposure to the temperature/density relationship for air and the associated convectional movement of air (hot air rises and cold air sinks); suggested completion of the activities Silver Spiral on page 4 and Full of Hot Air on page 7

PRE-ACTIVITY PREPARATION

Borrow the following two items from the junior high school or senior high school chemistry teacher (the results of the activity are well-worth the effort!): (1) an Erlenmeyer flask of a size that can sit on the bottom of a larger container (an aquarium tank or plastic sweater box, for example) and still be covered by several inches of water (flasks ranging in size between 300 mL and 600 mL are the most frequently used), and (2) a rubber, 2-hole stopper that fits the Erlenmeyer flask. You should insert two lengths of glass tubing or two lengths of plastic straw into the holes of the stopper so that they extend from the bottom of the stopper to about 2.5 cm (1 in.) above the top of the stopper. Your chemistry colleague will probably be glad to cut and insert the glass tubing or straw sections for you.

PROCESS SKILLS

Observing, inferring, hypothesizing

GROUP SIZE

Whole class

MATERIALS PER GROUP

- 1 large, clear container (aquarium tank or plastic sweater box, for example) (for teacher demonstration)
- Available water (for teacher demonstration)
- 1 pan for heating water (for teacher demonstration)
- 1 hot plate (for teacher demonstration)
- 1 small cooler of ice (for teacher demonstration)
- 4 or 5 marbles (for teacher demonstration)
- 1 Erlenmeyer flask (for teacher demonstration; see Pre-Activity Preparation)
- Red food coloring (for teacher demonstration)
- 1 prepared 2-hole rubber stopper (for teacher demonstration; see Pre-Activity Preparation)
- 1 oven mitt, potholder, or tongs (for teacher demonstration)

TEACHER INFORMATION

When water is heated, the motion of the water molecules increases. This, in turn, results in greater molecular spacing—the water expands. Consequently, there are fewer molecules per given volume of water than was the case prior to the heating. Fewer molecules mean that the volume of water has less mass or weight, or in other words, a decreased density.

(Density equals mass per volume.) Being less dense and lighter than surrounding cooler water (water that did not undergo heating), warm water rises. When water is cooled, the reverse process occurs: molecular motion and spacing decrease, density increases, and the denser, heavier water sinks. In lakes and (especially) in oceans, water motion associated with heating and cooling is very common; the convection that results forms a type of density current.

PROCEDURE

1. If necessary, review with students the relationship between air temperature, molecular spacing, and air density—including the vertical motions of air that accompany density differences: warm air, being less dense and lighter, rises; cold air, being denser and heavier, sinks. Remind students that such vertical motions of air are referred to as convection.

2. Ask students if they think convectional movement also occurs in water. Let students debate the question. Have them give reasons for their positions. *(Knowing that water, like air, is a fluid, it can be inferred that convection in water should be as commonplace as it is in air.)* Tell students that the purpose of today's activity is to investigate the answer to that question.

3. Have students gather around your work area so that all can see the demonstration. Set the large container at the center of view.

4. Put a pan of water on the hot plate to heat. It should contain enough water to completely fill the Erlenmeyer flask.

5. While the water is heating, fill the large container with cold tap water and then add plenty of ice. Also place 4 or 5 marbles in the Erlenmeyer flask. Hold the flask at an angle and gently roll the marbles in; do not drop them in or the flask might break. The purpose of the marbles is simply to add weight to the flask so that it will sit solidly on the bottom of the water-filled container.

6. Ask students questions such as the following:

   • What is happening to the density of the water that is being heated? Why? *(The density is decreasing; see Teacher Information.)*

   • What does this do to the weight of a given volume of the hot water? Why? *(It gets lighter; see Teacher Information.)*

   • What is happening to the density of the water to which ice was added? Why? *(The density is increasing; see Teacher Information.)*

   • What does this do to the weight of a given volume of the cold water? Why? *(It gets heavier; see Teacher Information.)*

7. Inform students of what you plan to do with the cold and hot water (see steps 8–10). Ask students each to develop a prediction detailing the outcome of the experiment with reference to movement or nonmovement of water. Have some of the students share their predictions with the class.

8. When the water is nearly boiling, add red food coloring to give it a deep color.

9. Fill the flask completely with the hot water. Observe caution; the water is very hot. Use an oven mitt, potholder, or tongs. Be careful not to splash hot water on yourself.

10. Insert the rubber stopper and carefully set the flask on the bottom of the large container. The flask will be hot! Use an oven mitt, potholder, or tongs. Make sure the tops of the glass tubes or straws are covered by several inches of ice-cold water. The final setup is shown in the accompanying illustration.

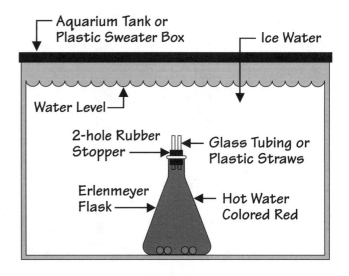

11. Students should closely observe the results. *(The hot red water will rise up through one of the tubes and enter the cold water. It will look like a smoke stack! Clear, cold water will descend through the other tube into the flask. The convection is very obvious. The convection and water reversal will continue for quite awhile—often for fifteen minutes or more. It is fun to watch.)*

(continues)

(continued)

12. As students observe the convection system in the water, ask questions such as:

    - What is the hot water doing? How do you know? *(Because it is less dense and light, it is rising out of the flask into the cold water as can be observed by the red color.)*

    - What is the cold water doing? How do you know? *(Because it is denser and heavier, it is sinking into the hotter water in the flask. This can be inferred because the red color of the hot flask water is becoming lighter or paler as it is mixed with clear, cold water.)*

    - Is this the same type of motion that would occur in air that was heated and cooled? *(yes)*

    - Does this illustrate that convection occurs in water and that water moves or flows due to differences in weight (density)? *(yes)*

EXTENSIONS AND ADAPTATIONS

1. Fill a clear plastic shoebox to about three-fourths with water. Put an immersion heater into the water at one end of the box and use tape to secure the top of the heater to the top edge of the box. Turn the heater on to high. Fill a zip-lock bag with ice cubes, adding marbles for weight. Put the bag into the water at the other end of the box and use tape to secure its top to the top edge of the box. When the heater is warm, use an eyedropper to add a few drops of red food coloring just below the water surface near the heater; observe the current motion. *(Water will rise and flow at the surface toward the ice.)* Add a few drops of blue food coloring just below the surface near the ice; observe the current motion. *(Water will sink and flow toward the heater along the bottom.)*

2. Related activities Silver Spiral on page 4, Full of Hot Air on page 7, Ahoy, Matey on page 58, and Are You Dense? on page 65.

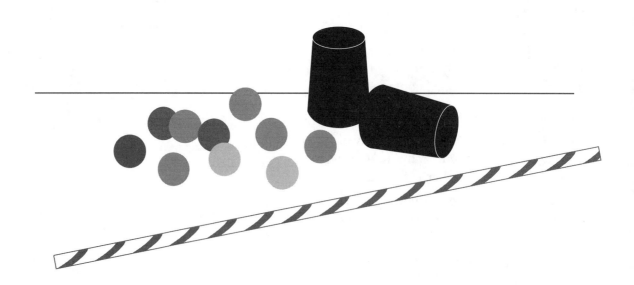

ARE YOU DENSE?

PRIMARY CONTENT

The formation of density currents (temperature, salinity, and turbidity currents)

PRIOR STUDENT KNOWLEDGE

Exposure to the concept of density

PRE-ACTIVITY PREPARATION

1. Prepare 4 containers of water of differing densities as follows: Put 946 mL (1 qt) of lukewarm tap water into each of 4 containers with wide openings (small pails or milk jugs with their tops cut off, for example). To one container, add 237 mL (1 c) of table salt; stir it well, and color it deep red with food coloring. Label the container Salty Water. To the second container, add about 237 mL (1 c) of soil and stir well. Label this container Muddy Water and keep it stirred during the activity. To the third container, add plenty of ice (keep ice in it throughout the activity) and color it deep blue with food coloring. Label this container Cold Water. Lastly, add green food coloring to the water in the fourth container. Label it Plain Tap Water.

2. Copy reproducible Student Observation Sheet (page 68), one copy per student.

PROCESS SKILLS

Observing, comparing, inferring, recording data, hypothesizing, identifying variables, experimenting

GROUP SIZE

2–4 students

MATERIALS PER GROUP

- 1 tall, clear container (2 L soda bottle or vegetable oil bottle, for example) about half filled with vegetable oil (for teacher demonstration)
- Table top
- 1 cup containing about 177 mL (6 oz) of water colored deep blue with food coloring (for teacher demonstration)
- 4 prepared and labeled containers of water (for whole class; see Pre-Activity Preparation)
- 1 tall clear wide-mouth plastic container (473 mL [16 oz] plastic cup, plastic peanut butter jar, or 2 L soda bottle with its top portion cut away, for example)
- Available room temperature water (for whole class)
- 1 plastic cup (any size) for rinsing the eyedropper between tests
- 1 small plastic cup for transporting water samples
- 1 copy of reproducible Student Observation Sheet for each student
- 1 eyedropper
- 1 sink or disposal bucket (for whole class)

TEACHER INFORMATION

There are two major categories of ocean currents: (1) drift currents, which are surface currents created by the frictional drag of prevailing winds blowing over the water surface; and (2) density currents (the focus of this activity), which flow as a result of differing densities of water—with denser, heavier water flowing downward (but not necessarily straight down as shown in the introductory demonstration) through less-dense,

(continues)

(continued)

lighter water. Consequently, density currents are subsurface currents. There are three types of density currents. A temperature current is colder water flowing through warmer water. Colder water is denser than warmer water because of the closer spacing between the slower-moving molecules of cold water (a decreased volume). A salinity current is saltier water flowing through less-saline water. The greater the salinity (amount of dissolved materials), the greater the density of water because dissolved materials add mass (weight) to the water. A turbidity current is muddier water flowing through clearer water. The greater the turbidity (amount of suspended materials), the greater the density of the water because suspended materials add mass (weight) to the water.

PROCEDURE

1. Introduce the activity by showing the class the tall container of vegetable oil but do not identify its contents. Do the same with the cup of blue-colored water. Have students gather around so that all can see.

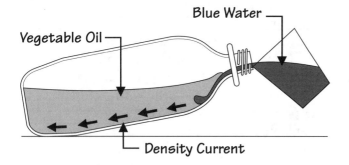

2. Set the base of the container of vegetable oil on a table. Tilt the container with one hand to a moderately low angle. With the other hand, slowly pour in the colored water. Blue globs of water will roll down the side of the inclined container beneath the yellow vegetable oil. Pour in spurts to get individual globs; pour continuously to get an unbroken stream. Now identify the liquids for the class.

3. Review what was observed by asking students questions such as:

   • Why did the blue water stay as a separate body and flow down to the bottom of the bottle beneath the yellow vegetable oil? Why didn't the two liquids just mix? *(To mix, liquids must be of similar density. Water is denser and heavier than oil. The water thus sunk beneath the lighter oil and flowed downhill under the influence of gravity.)*

   • Could the flow of water be considered a current even though the movement took place beneath the surface of the oil? *(certainly)*

   • Could such a subsurface current be created in the ocean or in lakes where there is only water and not water and oil? *(Yes it could if the masses of water were of significantly different densities. Do not tell students this, though. Most of them will probably answer no since they will likely be thinking in terms of differing fluids as opposed to differing densities.)*

4. Indicate to students that they will be investigating the answer to the last question in today's activity.

5. Group students and distribute the materials. Display and identify the 4 labeled containers of water but do not tell the class that the water is of differing densities.

6. Instruct each group to fill the tall, clear container with water to about three-fourths. Also have them fill the larger of the two plastic cups with water to about three-fourths to serve as rinse water for their eyedropper between each test. Indicate that the other plastic cup is for transporting water samples from the 4 containers at the front of the room.

7. It does not matter which water type a given group starts with. Students from each group should obtain a small amount (roughly 30 mL–59 mL [1 oz–2 oz]) of the selected water at the front of the room and transport it back to the group. You may wish to demonstrate to students the amount of water that should be in their transport cups.

8. On the Student Data Sheet, next to the type of water being tested, each student is to develop and record a prediction regarding what will happen when the test sample is dropped into the tall container of water.

9. Each group should take a dropperful of the sample from the transport cup. Students should place the end of the dropper against the inside of the tall container near the rim (above the water surface) and then release the sample by gently squeezing the dropper.

10. Each student is to observe what happens and record the results on the Student Data Sheet.

11. Groups should now do the following to prepare for testing the next water type: (a) clean the dropper inside and out in the rinse water; (b) dump in the sink or in the disposal bucket the water from the tall container and any of the sample remaining in the transport cup; (c) rinse out the transport cup with clean water; and (d) refill the tall container with clean water.

12. Groups should now repeat steps 7–11 for each of the remaining water types.

13. Conduct a session to review and discuss results. Include questions such as:

   • What were the results with the cold water? Why did it behave this way? *(It sank [flowed downward] through the regular water as a separate body because it was denser than the regular water to which it was added.)*

   • What were the results with the salty water? Why did it behave this way? *(same response)*

   • How about the muddy water? Why did it behave this way? *(same response)*

   • How about the plain tap water? Why did it behave this way? *(It mixed with the regular water as soon as it was added because both were of about the same density.)*

   • Do you think differences in muddiness, temperature, or salinity of ocean water might cause the denser water to flow as an ocean current? *(yes)*

   • Why is cold water denser than warmer water, muddy water denser than clear water, and salty water denser than less-salty water? (see Teacher Information)

14. Tell the students that the type of currents they created today are called density currents because they flow as a result of differing densities of water. Present additional information about density currents as desired (see Teacher Information).

EXTENSIONS AND ADAPTATIONS

Related activities Ahoy, Matey on page 58 and 'Round and 'Round She Goes on page 62.

ARE YOU DENSE? _____

STUDENT OBSERVATION SHEET

Name_____

Water Type	Prediction	Results
Muddy Water		
Plain Tap Water		
Salty Water		
Cold Water		

©Curriculum Associates, Inc.   *Earth Science Activities (KSAM)*

SHOOTING WATERS _____

PRIMARY CONTENT
- The concept of water pressure
- The relationship between depth and water pressure

PRIOR STUDENT KNOWLEDGE
No special prior knowledge is required.

PRE-ACTIVITY PREPARATION
1. Ask each student to bring from home a clean 2 L plastic soda bottle with the label removed.
2. Plan to do this activity outside on a nice day.

PROCESS SKILLS
Observing, comparing, inferring, measuring, hypothesizing, experimenting

GROUP SIZE
2–3 students

MATERIALS PER GROUP
- 1 ruler for each student
- 1 plastic soda bottle for each student
- 1 dark-colored marker for each student
- 1 compass point or medium-sized nail (can be restricted to teacher use only or, if you deem it safe and appropriate, distributed to each group; see notes in Procedure steps 3 and 6)
- Masking tape
- 1 sheet of paper
- 1 pencil
- Available water (for whole class)

TEACHER INFORMATION

Water is composed of H_2O molecules, each of which has mass or weight. Thus, due to its molecular composition, water has mass or weight. As a result of this weight, water exerts a force that is referred to as water pressure. The amount of water pressure is a function of water depth. As depth increases, so does water pressure (and vice versa). At greater depths, there is more water above, thus more weight, thus more pressure. Average atmospheric pressure at the surface is about 14.7 lb/in.^{2}. Since water is a fairly heavy substance, water pressure increases rapidly with depth—about 14.7 lb/in.^{2} for each 33 feet of depth. Thus at 100 feet down, water pressure is about

44 lb/in.^{2}; at the 10,000 foot depth, about 4,450 lb/in.^{2}; and at 25,000 feet, about 11,150 lb/in.^{2}. With these pressures, it is easy to understand why even a steel-hulled submarine will be crushed if it goes too deep.

PROCEDURE

1. Begin the activity by asking how many students have ever gone deep under the water in a swimming pool and experienced pain or an uncomfortable feeling in their ears. Inquire as to what they think causes that sensation.

2. Lead the discussion to the concept of water pressure (see Teacher Information). Discuss with students why water exerts pressure; do not, however, directly inform them of the relationship between water depth and the amount of water pressure. Tell students that they will be exploring water pressure in today's activity.

3. Group students and distribute the materials. Note: depending on the grade level and maturity of students, you may omit the compass point (or nail) from the group materials and handle it yourself (see step 6).

4. Direct students in each group to use a ruler and marking pen to draw a straight vertical line up the side of their bottle from the bottom to the base of the neck. This is most easily done if students within a group take turns holding each other's bottle stationary on a desk while one student draws the line. If the bottle has a dark sleeve around its base, the line may not show up on that section; tell students not to worry since this is of no consequence.

5. Direct each student to measure upward along the drawn line and mark an X on the line at each of the following points: 6.5 cm, 13 cm, and 19.5 cm if metric rulers are used—or $2\frac{1}{2}$ in., 5 in., and $7\frac{1}{2}$ in. if standard rules are used (see illustration).

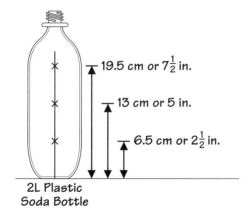

19.5 cm or $7\frac{1}{2}$ in.

13 cm or 5 in.

6.5 cm or $2\frac{1}{2}$ in.

2L Plastic
Soda Bottle

6. Have students punch holes in their bottles at the three marked points by inserting a compass point or nail fully into the bottle. (Note: if there is a question about students doing this task safely, you should punch all the holes.)

7. Students are to cover all 3 holes on their bottles with a single strip of masking tape. They should leave enough extra tape at the top end so that the tape can be folded under, creating a pull tab. Have students be sure that their tape is pressed down firmly along its entire length.

8. Outline for students the procedure for the remainder of the investigation (steps 10–14). Inform them that the distance the water shoots out of the holes will be dependent upon water pressure—the greater the pressure, the farther the horizontal distance of flow.

9. Then have each student develop and record on a sheet of paper a prediction regarding the outcome of the experiment—will the water shoot out to different distances from the 3 holes, or will all the distances be the same? If different, how will the holes rank in terms of distance of flow? Why?

10. Have each student now fill his/her bottle with water all the way up to the base of the neck.

11. Take the class outside.

12. One student in each group is to hold his/her bottle chest high, placing one hand under its base and one hand over its top. The bottle should be positioned so that the holes are pointed toward the student's immediate left or right, not toward or away from the student (see illustration). This position will allow the student to compare the horizontal distance of water flow from the holes when the tape is removed.

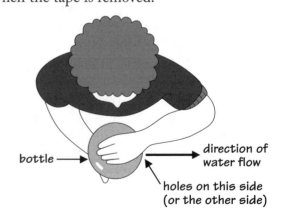

bottle

direction of
water flow

holes on this side
(or the other side)

13. A second member of each group is then to quickly pull the tape strip off the bottle. All members in the group should observe the results.

14. Have students repeat steps 12 and 13 until all students have tested their bottles.

15. Return to the classroom and discuss results. Include questions such as:

- Were the distances that the water shot out from the 3 holes the same or different? *(different)*

- From which hole did water shoot the greatest distance? The least distance? *(Water from the bottom hole would shoot the greatest distance; water from the top hole would shoot the least distance.)*

- How did these results compare with your prediction?

- What caused water to shoot out of the holes at different distances? Why? *(Water pressure was the cause. The different distances were a result of different amounts of water pressure— the greatest pressure being at the bottom hole and the least pressure at the top hole.)*

- What, then, controls the amount of water pressure? *(depth below the water surface—the greater the depth, the greater the water pressure; the less the depth, the less the water pressure)*

EXTENSIONS AND ADAPTATIONS

1. Allow students to observe while all the water drains from one of the bottles. After the first few seconds, have them concentrate on the bottom hole. They will see the horizontal distance of flow from that hole gradually decrease as the water depth (and pressure) in the bottles decreases.

2. Related activity A Squirty Contest on page 72.

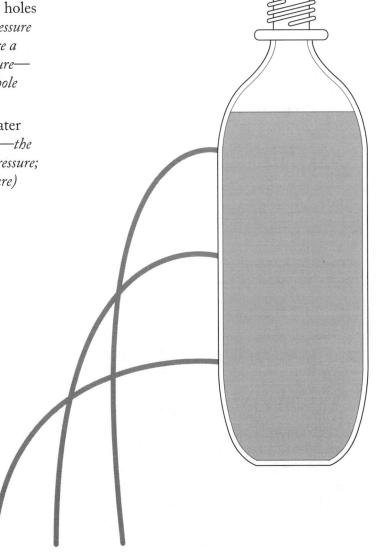

A SQUIRTY CONTEST

PRIMARY CONTENT

The relationship between water pressure and total volume of water

PRIOR STUDENT KNOWLEDGE

The concept of water pressure and its relationship to depth; suggested completion of the activity Shooting Waters on page 69

PRE-ACTIVITY PREPARATION

1. Each group will need a 2 L plastic soda bottle (one without the dark plastic sleeve around the bottom) and a small plastic soda bottle, any of the following common sizes: 355 mL (12 oz), 473 mL (16 oz), or 591 mL (20 oz). Have students bring both bottles from home.
2. Copy reproducible Student Data Sheet (page 75), one copy per student.
3. Plan to do this activity outside on a nice day.

PROCESS SKILLS

Observing, comparing, inferring, measuring, recording data, hypothesizing, identifying variables, experimenting

GROUP SIZE

2–4 students

MATERIALS PER GROUP

- 1 dark-colored marker
- 1 ruler
- 1 plastic soda bottle, 2 L
- 1 small plastic soda bottle
- 1 compass point or medium-sized nail (can be restricted to teacher use only or, if you deem it safe and appropriate, can be distributed to each group; see notes in Procedure steps 4 and 6)
- Masking tape
- 1 copy of reproducible Student Data Sheet for each student
- 1 measuring cup (can be made from a regular plastic cup by pouring in known amounts of water and then marking and labeling the different water levels)
- Available water (for whole class)
- 1 piece of chalk

TEACHER INFORMATION

Contrary to what most people think, the total volume of water has no bearing on water pressure. The primary influence on pressure is depth below the surface since that, in essence, controls how much weight is above a given point. The water pressure two feet under the surface in a bathtub or a swimming pool is the same as it is two feet under the surface in an ocean!

In this activity, immediately upon removal of the tape, water pressure is identical in the two bottles because the depth of the exit holes beneath the surface is the same in the two bottles. The result is streams of water of equal length. After a few seconds, however, the stream from the small bottle becomes shorter than that from the large bottle. Actually, both streams are decreasing in length, the one from the small bottle simply decreases faster than the one from the large bottle. This occurs because both bottles are losing water. This causes their water levels to drop, decreasing the distance (depth) between the surfaces and the holes. However, because the large bottle has a greater total volume of water, its water level does not lower nearly as fast as does the water level in the small bottle. Thus, water pressure does not decrease as rapidly in the large bottle as it does in the small. This variation is not addressed in the activity. However, you may choose to call it to the students' attention and discuss its cause.

PROCEDURE

1. Review with students the fact that there is a direct relationship between water pressure and depth below the water surface: the greater the depth, the greater the water pressure; the less the depth, the less the water pressure.

2. Ask students if they can think of any other things (variables), in addition to depth below the surface, that might affect water pressure. Responses might include water temperature, saltiness, muddiness, and motion. Indicate that these variables do have some influence on water pressure, but it is not significant. (See extension activity 1.)

3. It is unlikely that students will mention the total volume of water as a variable affecting water pressure. Suggest it and then explain what you mean through the questions such as the following:

   • Which has more water in it, a filled bathtub or an ocean? *(ocean)*

   • How would the water pressure compare at a depth of two feet below the surface in a bathtub and two feet below the surface of an ocean (water of the same depths but of very different volumes). (Allow debate but do not provide an answer. Indicate that the best way to solve the issue is to conduct an experiment.)

4. Group students and distribute the materials. (Note: depending on the grade level and maturity of students, you may choose to omit the compass point [or nail] from the group materials and handle it by yourself [see step 6].)

5. Direct each group to use a ruler and marking pen to carefully measure upward from the base of both bottles, marking an X at a height of 5 cm (2 in.) and a short horizontal line at a height of 12.7 cm (5 in.). This is most easily done if one member of the group holds a bottle stationary on a desk while other group members do the measuring and marking.

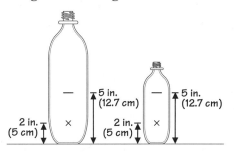

6. Have each group punch one hole in both bottles at the X points and then cover each hole with a piece of masking tape. Have students leave enough extra tape at the top end of each piece so that it can be folded under, creating a pull tab. Ask students to make sure that both pieces of tape are pressed down firmly over the holes. (Note: if the safety of the students is in question, you should punch all the holes.)

7. Outline for students the procedure for the remainder of the investigation (steps 8–12). Then have each student develop and record on the Student Data Sheet a prediction regarding the outcome of the experiment. (From which bottle [the one with the greater volume of water or the one with the lesser volume] will the water shoot out farthest—or, will the distances be the same?)

8. Each group should now fill both bottles with water to the marked horizontal line. Students should do the filling with a measuring cup so that the total amount (volume) of water in each bottle is known. Each student is to record these amounts on the Student Data Sheet in the Data Table; students should also record the depth of the hole beneath each water surface.

9. Take the class outside, preferably to a paved area. Each group needs to bring both bottles, a ruler, and chalk.

(continues)

(continued)

10. Have each group use chalk to draw a straight line on the pavement. (If pavement is not available, they can scratch a line in the soil or grass.) Students should place both bottles side-by-side, with the holes directly above the line that students marked, pointing in the same direction.

11. Students in each group should now quickly and simultaneously remove the tape over the holes on both bottles. Two students should each immediately put a finger on the pavement, one for each of the two streams of water. Holding these spots, the two students, along with the rest of the group, should observe the 2 streams of water.

12. When both flows have ceased, students should measure the distance between the marked line and each spot held by a finger. Each distance reflects the water pressure at the hole in the related bottle.

13. On returning to the classroom, have each student record the measured distances on the Student Data Sheet in the Data Table and then answer the questions on the sheet. Assist with reading as necessary; or you can verbally present the questions in the following discussion if students' lack of reading skills warrants.

14. Conduct a session to review results and discuss answers to the Student Data Sheet questions (see Teacher Information and Answer Key on page 154). The distances of water flow from the large and the small bottles should be essentially the same.

15. Discuss with students why there might have been small differences in the distances of the 2 streams (*inexact or incorrect measurements in the placement of the hole, the water line, the actual water level, and/or the distance of stream flow*).

EXTENSIONS AND ADAPTATIONS

1. It is possible that some of the variables that were suggested by students in step 2 of the Procedure may be subject to direct investigation. For example, you can test salinity differences by putting identical amounts of water in identical plastic bottles—with one amount of water being a prepared salt solution and the other being fresh water. You can test water pressure by punching holes at identical locations in both bottles and comparing the distances of the resulting streams. You can use the same approach with hot/cold water and clear/muddy water.

2. Have students do simple research on why submarines and bathyspheres are able to go so deep in the ocean without being crushed. Have students find out how deep an unprotected human can descend in water.

Earth Science Activities (KSAM)

A SQUIRTY CONTEST

STUDENT DATA SHEET

Name_____

Write your prediction for this investigation on the following lines.

_____

_____

_____

DATA TABLE

Container	Total Amount (Volume) of Water	Depth of Hole Below Water Surface	Distance of the Water Stream
Large Bottle			
Small Bottle			

1. Were the amounts (volumes) of water the same for both bottles? _____

2. If the answer to question 1 was no, which bottle had the most water? _____

_____

3. Was the depth of the hole below the water surface the same for each bottle? _____

4. When the tape was first removed, what was the water pressure at the hole in each bottle? (Circle the letter of the correct answer.)
   a. greater pressure in the large bottle
   b. greater pressure in the small bottle
   c. the same pressure in both bottles

5. Does the depth below the water surface affect how much water pressure there is?

_____

6. Does the total amount (volume) of water affect how much water pressure there is?

_____

WAVES IN A BOTTLE _____

PRIMARY CONTENT
- Introducing water waves
- Modeling waves

PRIOR STUDENT KNOWLEDGE

No special prior knowledge is required.

PRE-ACTIVITY PREPARATION

Have each student bring the following from home: a small bottle of vegetable oil and a clear 2 L plastic soda bottle (with cap); the bottle should be clean, with the label removed. Each student will need about 0.5 L (17 oz) of the vegetable oil; you can send the remainder back home or store it for future use.

PROCESS SKILLS

Observing, inferring, experimenting

GROUP SIZE

Individual

MATERIALS PER GROUP
- 1 clear 2 L plastic soda bottle with cap
- Available water (for whole class)
- Food coloring (choice of colors)
- Approximately 0.5 L (17 oz) of vegetable oil
- Several paper towels

TEACHER INFORMATION

Due to their differing densities, oil and water are immiscible and do not mix. This results in a density interface between the two fluids in the wave bottle. It is along this interface that waves and turbulence occur as energy is applied to the bottle. Waves, therefore, represent energy in motion. The wave form of the energy becomes visible because of the movement of the material through which the energy is traveling. Since energy flow tends to be concentrated along density interfaces, most ocean (or lake or bathtub) waves occur along the surface—at the atmosphere/water interface. Four basic characteristics of water waves are: (1) crest—the high point of the wave, (2) trough—the low point of the wave, (3) wavelength—the horizontal distance between two successive crests, and (4) wave height—the vertical distance between the crest and the trough.

PROCEDURE

1. Begin the activity by asking students if they have ever taken a really close look at water waves—perhaps in a pond, lake, the ocean, or even the bathtub. Pretend that a friendly alien from a waterless planet has landed in the schoolyard. Select a student to play this role. Because the alien has never seen water waves, ask for volunteers to describe waves to the alien.

2. Tell the class that different parts or properties of waves are named to allow easier description and communication. Draw a cross section of some simple waves on the chalkboard and explain to the class these four basic wave characteristics: crest, trough, wavelength, and wave height (see illustration and Teacher Information).

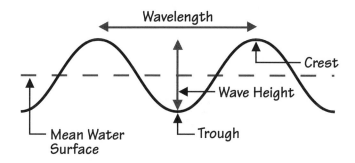

3. Inform students that water waves come in all sizes—from tiny little ripples like those seen in a bathtub or puddle to giant waves with long wavelengths and wave heights so great that they can tower over ships.

4. Ask students if they would like to study waves a little closer by each making a wave bottle—a simple device for observing wave properties and some very beautiful wave motions.

5. Distribute materials to each student.

6. Instruct students each to fill their bottle to about three-fourths with water. They should add food coloring in an amount sufficient to give the water a good deep color. Any color will work, although blue and red are the most popular. Let students make their own color choices. Students can each cap their bottle and shake it to mix the coloring.

7. Ask students each to slowly fill the remainder of the bottle with vegetable oil to the very top of the rim so that no air whatsoever remains in the bottle. It is better to overfill a little and clean up any excess with a paper towel than it is to underfill. Assist students with this step as necessary.

8. Pouring the oil into the water creates air bubbles in the oil. For best results, upon completion of step 7, students should leave their bottles standing and uncapped until all the air bubbles have dissipated—usually about an hour or so. When all the air bubbles are gone, students can add a little more oil, if necessary, to completely fill their bottles.

9. Students should tightly cap their bottles. The wave bottles are now complete.

10. The bottles can be used in a variety of ways for wave study and observation—or just for enjoyment! For example, direct each student to hold the bottle horizontally and rock it up and down like a seesaw. Let each turn the bottle upside-down, both slowly and rapidly. Let each hold the bottle horizontally on the desk and apply energy by thumping the base of the bottle soundly with the heel of the hand or with a book.

11. The result is slow-motion wave action and/or turbulence along the density interface between the oil and water. It's great fun, it's beautiful, and the students will love it!

12. Give students ample time to play and experiment with the bottles. Challenge them to try to come up with innovative motions of their own.

13. Find out whether, through their investigations, students have picked up on the fact that for waves to be created inside the bottles, energy must in some way be transferred to the bottles and thus to the liquids in the bottles—the energy might be from thumping, shaking, rocking, or whatever. Lead students to understand that waves are actually energy in transfer—energy made visible by the movement of the material through which the energy is traveling.

14. Allow students to take their wave bottles home to show their families and friends.

EXTENSIONS AND ADAPTATIONS

1. This activity is appropriate for use in a learning center.

2. Let students take their bottles to other classrooms to demonstrate wave motion.

3. Students can also make mini wave bottles with small, clear plastic soda bottles.

4. Let students experiment with a slinky to produce waves in solid material. This can lead to a discussion of earthquakes—the result of energy waves passing through the solid earth.

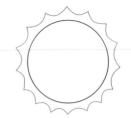

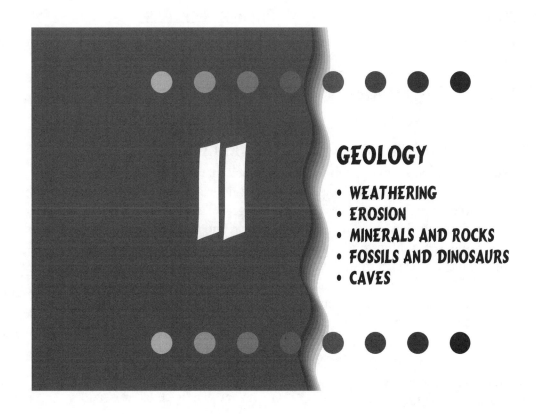

GEOLOGY

- WEATHERING
- EROSION
- MINERALS AND ROCKS
- FOSSILS AND DINOSAURS
- CAVES

GOOD-BYE ROCK— SHAKE, RATTLE, AND ROLL

PRIMARY CONTENT

Understanding abrasion as a weathering agent in flowing water

PRIOR STUDENT KNOWLEDGE

No special prior knowledge is required.

PRE-ACTIVITY PREPARATION

1. Obtain small-sized gravel, small enough to pass easily through the neck of a 2 L soda bottle. You will need enough to supply each group with approximately 475 mL (2 c). Most gravel is composed of limestone, and this is preferable; however, almost any composition (except chart) will do. You can obtain gravel at concrete supply companies and at most garden supply centers.
2. Wash the gravel thoroughly by placing it in a colander, rising and stirring repeatedly.
3. For each group, place about 237 mL (1 c) of the clean gravel in each of two 2 L plastic soda bottles and then cap them. Using a funnel will make this an easy task.

PROCESS SKILLS

Observing, comparing, inferring, identifying variables, experimenting

GROUP SIZE

2–5 students

MATERIALS PER GROUP

- Rock material, in a range of sizes, for example: a pinch or two of sand, a few pieces of gravel, a golf-ball-size rock, a baseball-size rock, and a cantaloupe-size rock
- 1 cookie sheet (for teacher demonstration)
- 1 pitcher of water (for teacher demonstration)
- 1 long pan or sink (for teacher demonstration)
- 2 plastic soda bottles, 2 L, (capped), each containing about 237 mL (1 c) of clean gravel
- Masking tape
- Available water (for whole class)
- 2 clear plastic cups (any size)
- 1 hand lens

TEACHER INFORMATION

Weathering is the breakdown of rock material; erosion is the removal or transport of the weathered debris or sediment. Additional weathering may occur during erosion. Agents of weathering are commonly divided into two categories: physical and chemical. Physical agents are those that mechanically break rock into smaller sizes. Such agents include ice wedging, temperature changes, plant wedging, and abrasion. Chemical weathering occurs when a rock is changed into a different chemical substance.

This activity addresses abrasion, an extremely important weathering process that takes place during wind, water, and glacial transport. Abrasion is the physical breakdown of rock that occurs as rocks in transport hit and scrape against each other and/or against the surface over which they are being moved. Consequently, not only can the rocks in transport be abraded (as in this activity), but so can the rock surfaces over which the sediment moves. This activity concentrates on abrasion during sediment transport by water.

PROCEDURE

1. Start the activity by showing the class the cantaloupe-size rock. Ask, "Where do rocks of this size come from?" Lead students to the conclusion that they come from the breakdown of even larger rocks, perhaps the size of a basketball or a desk.

2. Then show students the baseball-size rock and repeat the question. *(They come from the breakdown of, perhaps, cantaloupe-size rocks.)* Continue the sequence with the remaining materials down to sand, which comes from the breakdown of, perhaps, gravel-size material.

3. Lead students to understand that the breakdown of rock, called weathering, is a natural process operating on earth. Through weathering, rocks are gradually and continually broken down into smaller and smaller sizes, from solid bedrock (the crust) to automobile-size boulders and so on down to material even much smaller than sand grains (see table).

ROCK MATERIAL SIZES	
Size Name	Diameter (mm)
Clay	<0.002
Silt	0.002 to 0.02
Sand	0.02 to 2
Pebbles	2 to 64
Cobbles	64 to 256
Boulders	>256
Bedrock	Continuous

4. Ask students if they think small rocks can be moved or carried by flowing water. To demonstrate that they can be, lay several pieces of gravel toward one end of a cookie sheet. Lift that end of the cookie sheet to create an inclined plane, but not to the point that the gravel slides. The lower end of the plane should be over a pan or sink.

5. Pour water at the top of the plane and let the class observe the water flowing downward, moving gravel with it. Ask students questions such as:

   - Can rocks be carried by flowing water? *(yes)*

   - Do you think this happens in nature? *(Yes, material can be transported by rivers, streams, and ocean currents; and material can be moved back and forth over a beach by waves.)*

   - Would the movement of rocks within flowing water cause them to break down into smaller sizes? Indicate that the purpose of today's activity is to investigate the answer to this question.

6. Group students and distribute the materials. Inform groups that the gravel in all the bottles is the same and has been thoroughly cleaned. It is important that students accept these facts.

7. Have each group use masking tape to label one bottle 1000 Shakes and the other bottle No Shakes. They should then fill both bottles with water to about one-third and cap them tightly.

8. All students within a group are to take turns shaking the 1000 Shakes bottle *vigorously* 100 times each until the bottle has been shaken a total of 1000 times. They should leave the No Shakes bottle undisturbed. This step is noisy, but fun! If you wish, you can have the shaking done outdoors.

9. Immediately after the 1000 shakes have been completed, instruct groups to pour water from the shaken bottle into a clear plastic cup to about three-fourths and then pour water from the No Shakes bottle into the second cup to about three-fourths. Students are then to compare the 2 cups of water for several minutes.

(continues)

(continued)

10. Pose questions such as the following:

    - What is the water and gravel in the 1000 Shakes bottle a model of? *(rocks being moved about in flowing or moving water)*

    - How did the 2 samples of water taken from the bottles compare? *(The water from the shaken bottle looked very dirty; the water from the unshaken bottle was clean.)*

    - Could the one sample be dirty because the gravel in the bottle was dirty? *(No; the gravel in both bottles was very clean when the experiment was started. Also, if dirty gravel was the cause, the water from the unshaken bottle would also have been dirty, and it wasn't.)*

    - Then what could have caused the water in the shaken bottle to get so dirty? *(Because the rocks were in motion within the moving water, the rocks were hitting and rubbing against one another. This contact caused little pieces to chip off the rocks. All those tiny pieces made the water dirty.)*

    - How do you know for sure that it was tiny pieces chipped off the moving rocks that made the water dirty? *(After a few minutes, the tiny pieces began to settle to the bottom of the cup, forming a layer of sediment.)*

    - How do you know for sure it was the hitting and rubbing that caused the breakdown—couldn't it have been just the effect of the water on the rocks? *(No; the rocks in the unshaken bottle were also in water, but they were not affected.)*

11. Inform students that the breakdown of rock they observed in the investigation is called abrasion, one of the most important of the weathering agents. It occurs while rocks are being transported by water (as modeled in this activity), by wind, or by glaciers.

12. Have each group remove 3 or 4 pieces of gravel from each bottle and observe them with a hand lens. Students should notice some rounding of the corners and edges of the rocks in the shaken sample as a result of chips having been removed. (Note that rounded refers to the lack of sharp corners and edges and does not necessarily mean spherical.) Students will not observe rounding with the unshaken rocks. Students may also see evidence of scratching and scraping on the shaken rocks. This phenomenon will be even more observable if the bottles are shaken 2000 times instead of 1000.

EXTENSIONS AND ADAPTATIONS

1. Remove some gravel from one of the 1000 Shakes bottles and save it for later comparison. Then leave the bottle out for the entire year. Set up a schedule with a different student shaking the bottle 100 times before or after school each day. At the end of the year, remove some of the gravel and compare it with the saved sample. The difference will be amazing!

2. Have students collect rocks from creek beds during periods of low water and then observe how abrasion has caused them to be exceptionally smooth and rounded.

3. Related activities Groovy Glacier on page 83, Plant Power on page 86, Ice Is Nice Unless You're a Rock on page 89, and Rock Fizz on page 92.

GROOVY GLACIER

PRIMARY CONTENT

- Understanding abrasion as an agent of weathering in glaciers
- Introducing glaciers

PRIOR STUDENT KNOWLEDGE

The general concept of weathering and the concept of abrasion during the transport of rocks by water and wind; suggested completion of the activity Good-bye Rock—Shake, Rattle, and Roll on page 80

PRE-ACTIVITY PREPARATION

1. Each group will need 5–15 angular (not smooth and rounded) rocks of grape-to-walnut size to spread across the bottom of one of the containers identified in the materials listing. You can collect rocks, you can get them at concrete supply companies as coarse (large) gravel, or you can obtain them as rock mulch at garden centers.
2. Using old boxes, cut a 30 cm x 46 cm (12 in. x 18 in.) piece of corrugated cardboard for each group.
3. Obtain pictures of glaciers and glacial striations and grooves in bedrock from sources such as encyclopedias or geology and earth science books.

4. Arrange to use the cafeteria freezer. You can start the activity in the afternoon after cafeteria personnel have finished and complete it the next morning.

PROCESS SKILLS

Observing, comparing, inferring, hypothesizing, experimenting

GROUP SIZE

2–4 students

MATERIALS PER GROUP

- Several pictures of glaciers and glacial grooves and striations (for whole class)
- 5–15 angular rocks (see Pre-Activity Preparation)
- 2 large whipped-topping containers or large margarine tubs
- Available water (for whole class)
- Masking tape
- 1 freezer (for whole class)
- Paper towels
- 1 piece of corrugated cardboard (see Pre-Activity Preparation)

TEACHER INFORMATION

This activity addresses abrasion, an extremely important weathering process that takes place during wind, water, and glacial transport. Abrasion is the physical weathering (breakdown) of rock that occurs as rocks in transport hit and scrape against one

another and/or against the surface over which they are being moved. Consequently, not only can the rocks in transport be abraded, but, as shown in this activity, so can the rock surface over which the sediment moves. This activity concentrates on abrasion resulting from glacial movement.

(continues)

(continued)

Glaciers form when, over a long period of time, more snow falls during the winter than can melt during the summer. The result is a continued thickening of the snow layer. As it thickens, the pressure produced by the weight of the overlying snow causes underlying snow to change to ice. With continued thickening, the mass of ice and snow begins to flow outward under its own weight, much like a glob of thick honey spreads outward as more honey is added to the glob. This is the only mechanism of movement for the great continental glaciers or ice sheets. With alpine glaciers, that force is aided by gravity as the glaciers move down valleys.

During glacial movement, there is a great deal of frictional melting and refreezing at the bottom of the glacier, resulting in rocks being frozen into the glacier's base. This, in turn, makes glaciers the most effective abrading force in nature—their bottoms are akin to giant files or pieces of coarse sandpaper—scraping, gouging, and scratching everything they move over! Thus, both the rocks in the glacier's base and the surface over which the glacier moves are heavily abraded.

PROCEDURE

1. If necessary, review with students the concept of weathering, particularly the process of abrasion as rock particles are transported by water or wind. Then ask students if they can think of any other ways abrasion can take place. If students do not suggest it, indicate that glaciers are a good possibility.

2. Explain what a glacier is, how it is formed, and how rocks become captured and encased at its base (see Teacher Information). Supplement the discussion with pictures of glaciers.

3. Ask students to predict how glacial movement results in abrasion to the rocks at the glacier's base and, especially, abrasion to the surface over which the glacier moves (see Teacher Information.) Then tell students that, in order to test their predictions, they will begin an activity to model glaciers.

4. Group students and distribute the materials. It is suggested that you have the rocks in a container where they can be obtained by groups as needed.

5. Instruct groups to obtain 5–10 rocks to start off with. Students are to spread the rocks evenly across the bottom of one of their containers. Students can obtain more rocks as needed for this task. For best results, it is suggested: (a) that students leave some space between most of the rocks for water to occupy and freeze; (b) if possible, that students place the most jagged side (as opposed to a flat side) of a rock down; and (c) if there are any elongated rocks, that students place or position at least some of them vertically so that they will be encased deeper in the ice. See the first illustration, representing the best type of placement.

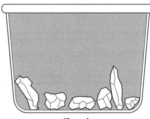 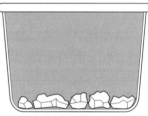

Rock Arrangement #1 (better results)   Rock Arrangement #2 (reduced results)

6. Have groups use masking tape to label both containers with the group members' initials. Students should then fill the containers with water to about three-fourths and carefully transport them to the freezer.

7. Groups are to retrieve their containers the next day. They should let the containers stand at room temperature until the water in the container with rocks has melted enough to expose about 3 mm–6 mm ($\frac{1}{8}$ in.–$\frac{1}{4}$ in.) of the edges of the rocks at the container's base.

8. Instruct groups to remove both the ice blocks, set them on paper towels, and observe them, especially the sides. Explain that the block with rocks encased in its base is a good model of an actual glacier.

9. Students should then rub both ice blocks across the cardboard section, with one student holding the cardboard in place. The cardboard models the bedrock over which glaciers move. Since glaciers are unimaginably heavy, they exert a tremendous downward force. To represent this force, tell students to push down heavily on the ice blocks as they push them across the cardboard.

10. Students are to observe the effect that the movement of the blocks had on the cardboard's surface. Students can take turns pushing the ice blocks until all have participated.

11. Conduct a session to review and discuss results. Include questions such as:

    • What effect did the ice block with no rocks in it have on the surface? *(little or none)*

    • What effect did the ice block with rocks (glacier model) have on the surface? *(Scrapes, tears, and scratches would be easily visible.)*

    • What might the bottom of a glacier be compared to? *(a giant file or piece of coarse sandpaper)*

    • Do you see now what an actual glacier can do to the rock surface over which it moves?

    • What do we call the process by which rock is broken down by scraping, grinding, and hitting against another rock? *(abrasion, a type of physical weathering)*

    • Do you think rocks transported in water or wind abrade the surface over which they are moving as much as a glacier does? *(Wind-blown material does so more than water-carried material, but neither have as much impact on the surface as glaciers do.)*

12. Display the pictures showing actual surface features (grooves and striations) created by glacial abrasion.

EXTENSIONS AND ADAPTATIONS

1. If you can obtain sections of drywall, it is even better for showing the effects of glacial abrasion than is corrugated cardboard. Check with a drywall contractor who may be willing to supply you with scrap pieces of drywall.

2. Related activities Good-bye Rock—Shake, Rattle, and Roll on page 80, Plant Power on page 86, Ice Is Nice Unless You're a Rock on page 89, and Rock Fizz on page 92.

PLANT POWER

PRIMARY CONTENT
Plant wedging as an agent of weathering

PRIOR STUDENT KNOWLEDGE
No special prior knowledge is required.

PRE-ACTIVITY PREPARATION
1. Obtain packaged garden-variety green bean, navy bean, or pea seeds—enough to supply the amount called for in step 6 of the Procedure.
2. Prepare the seeds for germination by placing them in a shallow pan lined with several layers of wet paper towels; leave them overnight.
3. Read the CAUTION note in step 6 of the Procedure.

PROCESS SKILLS
Observing, comparing, inferring, hypothesizing, experimenting

GROUP SIZE
2–3 students

MATERIALS PER GROUP
- 1 small, empty match box with slide-on cover
- 1 small section of aluminum foil, enough to line the inside of the match box
- 1 small section of blotter paper, enough to line the bottom of the match box
- Scissors
- Available water (for whole class)
- 1 plastic cup (any size) for transporting water
- Presoaked seeds (for whole class; see Pre-Activity Preparation)
- 1 paper towel
- 1 zip-lock sandwich bag
- 1 small strip of masking tape
- 1 sheet of paper for each student
- 1 pencil for each student

TEACHER INFORMATION
Weathering is the breakdown of rock material into smaller sizes; erosion is the removal or transport of the weathered debris or sediment. Additional weathering may occur during erosion. Agents of weathering are commonly divided into two categories: physical and chemical. Physical agents are those that mechanically break the rock into smaller sizes. Such agents include ice wedging, temperature changes, plant wedging, and abrasion. Chemical weathering occurs when a rock is changed into a different chemical substance.

This activity addresses plant wedging. Chemical and physical weathering of rock often result in the accumulation of some of the fine weathered material (soil) in the cracks of rock; and/or the cracks may serve as catches for weathered material being transported by wind or water. Plant seeds, also carried by wind, water, or gravity (falling from above), may also lodge in the cracks. The subsequent growth of plants and their root systems produces tremendous forces that are capable of breaking and moving rock. The larger the size of the plant, the greater its plant-wedging force. Plant wedging is a slow process in nature, normally observable only after months or years. This activity attempts to speed up the process for student observation and investigation.

PROCEDURE

1. Prime the class for the activity by generating discussion through questions such as those that follow. Do not, however, provide answers or content information at this time.

   - Have you ever seen plants growing from cracks in rock, concrete, or pavement? Out of the rock walls of a road cut? Ask students who have seen such occurrences to describe their observations.

   - Since there doesn't appear to be any soil, how do plants grow in such places? How did they get there in the first place?

   - Do you think such plants affect the rock in any way? How?

   - Do you think plants and plant roots have any power to push on, move, or break other materials, including solid rock? Tell students that today they will begin an activity to investigate the answer to this question.

2. Group students and distribute the materials. Have students in each group slide the cover off the match box and set the cover aside until later.

3. Instruct each group to fully line the inside of the match box with a single sheet of foil so that there are no breaks or seams in the lining. With a little pushing and bending, the foil can be made to conform tightly to the shape of the box. The foil should also fold over the edges of the box (see illustration).

4. Students should cut and place a section of blotter paper in the bottom of the box over the foil lining (see illustration). The fit does not have to be perfect.

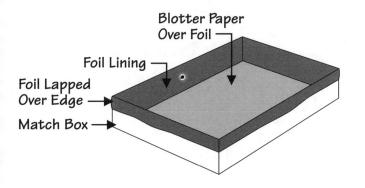

Blotter Paper Over Foil
Foil Lining
Foil Lapped Over Edge
Match Box

5. Direct each group to obtain a small amount of water and fully saturate the blotter paper.

6. Distribute to each group enough of the presoaked seeds to completely cover the bottom of the box. Students should then cover the seeds with a water-saturated piece of paper towel. Again, the fit does not have to be perfect. CAUTION: because most garden-variety seeds are pretreated with a fungicide, warn students against putting the seeds in their mouths; also, require that students wash their hands after handling the seeds.

7. Have each group replace the cover on the match box, carefully place the box in the sandwich bag, and then seal the bag. Ask students to write group members' initials on a small strip of masking tape and attach it to the outside of the bag for identification purposes.

8. Each group should now move their bag to a warm, dark (as possible) place in the room where it can remain undisturbed for one to two weeks, depending on room conditions.

9. Require each student to develop and record on a sheet of paper a prediction about what will happen to the seeds and the match box and whether there will be any evidence of plant power.

10. Allow students to observe and discuss their setups daily. Stems and roots of the germinating seeds will gradually fill the box and begin to exit through space between the box and cover. The boxes, in turn, should show increasing evidence of the force exerted by outward pushing roots and stems—bulging or swelling and possibly even splitting along the seams.

11. When all evidence of growth has ceased, let groups retrieve their boxes and remove them from the sandwich bags for a close look. Have students infer what would happen if the seeds were in the cracks of rock or pavement and what the force of a large plant, such as a tree, is capable of. As an example, inform students that cities often have problems with tree roots breaking or lifting up entire sections of sidewalks, curbs, and driveways.

12. Discuss the process of weathering and the important role of plants as weathering agents (see Teacher Information).

EXTENSIONS AND ADAPTATIONS

1. This activity is appropriate for use in a learning center.

2. If an actual example of plant wedging (lifted sidewalk or broken curb, for example) is nearby, take the class on a walk to directly observe the phenomenon.

3. Wrap presoaked garden-variety bean seeds individually in water-saturated blotter paper. Make a paste of plaster of Paris in a small, shallow container (a cut-down plastic foam cup, for example). Insert several wrapped beans in the plaster so that they are barely covered (not too deep!). The blotter-paper folds should be to the top. Set the cup in a warm location and observe as the germinating seeds break through solid rock (dried plaster) in about five to ten days.

4. Related activities Good-bye Rock—Shake, Rattle, and Roll on page 80, Groovy Glacier on page 83, Ice Is Nice Unless You're a Rock on page 89, and Rock Fizz on page 92.

ICE IS NICE UNLESS YOU'RE A ROCK _____

PRIMARY CONTENT
Ice wedging as an agent of weathering

PRIOR STUDENT KNOWLEDGE
No special prior knowledge is required.

PRE-ACTIVITY PREPARATION
You will need a freezer for both parts of this activity. Make arrangements to use the cafeteria freezer. You can start each part of the activity in the afternoon after cafeteria personnel have finished and then complete it the next morning.

PROCESS SKILLS
Observing, comparing, inferring, hypothesizing, experimenting

GROUP SIZE
2–4 students

MATERIALS PER GROUP
- 1 clean milk carton, 237 mL ($\frac{1}{2}$ pt) or 473 mL (1 pt)
- Masking tape
- Available water (for whole class)
- 1 stapler (one or more to be shared by the whole class)
- Paper towels
- 1 sheet of paper for each student
- 1 pencil for each student
- 1 freezer (for whole class)
- 1 clean aluminum soda can, 355 mL (12 oz)

TEACHER INFORMATION

Weathering is the breakdown of rock material into smaller sizes; erosion is the removal or transport of the weathered debris or sediment. Additional weathering may occur during erosion. Agents of weathering are commonly divided into two categories: physical and chemical. Physical agents are those that mechanically break the rock into smaller sizes. Such agents include ice wedging, temperature changes, plant wedging, and abrasion. Chemical weathering occurs when a rock is changed into a different chemical substance.

This activity focuses on ice wedging. Upon freezing, the volume of water expands by 10%–12% because the water molecules align into solid crystalline shapes which require greater molecular spacing. This expansion force is quite strong and is capable of breaking and splitting rock when water gets trapped or semiconfined in both large and small cracks in the rock. Ice wedging is one of the more important of the physical weathering agents, although it is limited to climates experiencing subfreezing temperatures.

PROCEDURE

Part One: Ice Wedging Milk Cartons

1. Introduce the activity by asking students how many different sizes of rocks they have seen. Depending on location, their descriptions may range from large boulders to grains of sand.

2. Inform the class that most rocks start out as massive, solid, continuous bedrock (the crust), which, in essence, represents one giant rock—the earth! For there to be individual rocks of sizes smaller than this, rock must be broken down or fragmented.

3. Lead students to understand that the breakdown of rock, a process called weathering, is a natural process operating on the earth. Through weathering, rocks are gradually and progressively broken down into smaller and smaller sizes, from solid bedrock (the crust) all the way down to material much smaller than grains of sand (see table).

ROCK MATERIAL SIZES	
Size Name	Diameter (mm)
Clay	<0.002
Silt	0.002 to 0.02
Sand	0.02 to 2
Pebbles	2 to 64
Cobbles	64 to 256
Boulders	>256
Bedrock	Continuous

4. Ask students if they think water can play a role in the weathering of rocks and, if so, how. The question refers to the breakdown of rocks, not the movement or transport of rocks (erosion). After students have expressed their ideas, indicate that the purpose of today's activity is to investigate answers to that question.

5. Group students and distribute the milk cartons and masking tape. Have students in each group write group members' initials on the tape and attach it to the carton for purposes of identification.

6. Have each group fill its carton completely with water—all the way to the rim of the spout. Students should then close the carton and staple it shut. If it is filled properly (to the spout rim), some water will be forced out when the carton is closed; students can wipe this up with paper towels.

7. Each student is to develop and record on a sheet of paper a prediction as to what will happen after the carton has been left in the freezer overnight.

8. Carefully transport the cartons to the freezer, put them in, and leave them there overnight. Have groups retrieve their cartons the following day.

9. Ask each group to observe, describe, and discuss the effects of freezing water on its carton. (a bulged or swollen shape and, very frequently, splitting along the top or the seams)

10. Discuss with students the fact that when water freezes, its volume expands (see Teacher Information). This expansion produces a strong outward force on any material or object that is containing the water—as observed with the milk cartons in this activity.

Part Two: Ice Wedging Soda Cans

1. Tell the class, "As we all just observed, ice expansion is strong enough to swell and split a milk carton; but milk cartons are composed of cardboard. Do you think the force produced by freezing water is strong enough to do the same thing to a metal container?"

2. Distribute an aluminum soda can to each group. Students should attach identification labels as in step 5 of Part One.

3. Have each group fill its can completely with water—all the way to the tab opening. Even a little standing water in the recessed top of the can is okay.

4. Each student should again develop and record on a sheet of paper a prediction as in step 7 of Part One.

5. Carefully transport the cans to the freezer, put them in, and leave them there overnight. Ask groups to retrieve their cans the following day.

6. Have groups observe, describe, and discuss the effects of freezing water on their cans. (*All the cans will look bulged and swollen even though they are composed of metal; typically, 50%–75% of the cans will be split down the side!* [Note: if you can leave the cans in the freezer for as long as twenty-four hours, this will increase their chances of splitting.])

7. Ask students to infer what might happen if water fills cracks and cavities in rock and then freezes. Indicate that the breaking of rock that frequently results is called ice wedging, one of the important agents of physical weathering (see Teacher Information).

EXTENSIONS AND ADAPTATIONS

1. If a freezer is not available in your school, you can assign this activity as a home project.

2. In areas that have subfreezing winters, have students look for examples of ice wedging in bluffs and road cuts.

3. As a whole-class demonstration, cut the top half off a 1.89 L (½ gal) cardboard milk carton and coat the inside with non-stick vegetable spray. Pour in a thin 1.3 cm (½ in.) layer of plaster of Paris. Inflate a very small round balloon so that it fits into the carton with about a 6 mm–13 mm (¼ in.–½ in.) clearance on the sides and top. Tie the balloon off and coat it with vegetable spray. Holding the balloon nozzle upward, pour more plaster of Paris in the carton so that it completely encases the balloon, leaving only the nozzle sticking out. After the plaster has hardened, prick the nozzle and pull the now-deflated balloon through the nozzle opening in the plaster. Remove the sides of the milk carton. You now have a hard rock with a cavity inside. Fill the cavity completely with water, put the rock inside a larger container, and place the setup in the freezer. Within twelve to twenty-four hours, the class will be able to observe the breaking power of ice wedging—even against solid rock!

4. Related activities Good-bye Rock—Shake, Rattle, and Roll on page 80, Groovy Glacier on page 83, Plant Power on page 86, and Rock Fizz on page 92.

ROCK FIZZ

PRIMARY CONTENT

The concept of chemical weathering

PRIOR STUDENT KNOWLEDGE

Previous exposure to the concepts of physical and chemical changes in materials is helpful but not mandatory.

PRE-ACTIVITY PREPARATION

1. Each group will need about 8–10 small (acorn-size or smaller) pieces of limestone. Limestone gravel works well, or you may choose to break pieces off a larger rock or outcrop. You can obtain gravel from concrete supply companies or most garden centers, but be sure it's limestone gravel. If necessary, you can substitute for limestone decorative marble chips (available at garden centers, but more expensive).
2. Clean the limestone pieces by placing them in a colander and rising them with water.

PROCESS SKILLS

Observing, comparing, inferring

GROUP SIZE

2–3 students

MATERIALS PER GROUP

- 8–10 small pieces of limestone
- 1 bottle, 3.79 L (1 gal), of 5% white vinegar (for whole class)
- Masking tape
- Available water (for whole class)
- 2 clear plastic cups, 177 mL–355 mL (6 oz–12 oz)

TEACHER INFORMATION

Weathering is the breakdown of rock material into smaller sizes; erosion is the removal or transport of the weathered debris or sediment. Additional weathering may occur during erosion. Agents of weathering are commonly divided into two categories: physical and chemical. Physical agents are those that mechanically break rock into smaller sizes. Such agents include ice wedging, temperature changes, plant wedging, and abrasion. Chemical weathering, the focus of this activity, occurs when a rock is changed into a different chemical substance.

Many natural acids exist in nature. One of the best examples is precipitation. When rain occurs, carbon dioxide in the atmosphere dissolves into the falling raindrops, creating a weak carbonic acid with a pH of between 5 and 5.6 (on the pH scale, 7 is neutral, and 0 is the most acidic). For comparison, some soft drinks with a pH of around 3.0 are much more acidic than rain. Certain rock types (those composed of calcium carbonate), especially limestone and marble, react chemically with carbonic acid and thus undergo chemical weathering. In industrialized areas, rain may absorb various sulfur emissions and form sulfuric acid, which is significantly more acidic than the naturally occurring carbonic acid. Such acid rain is a major issue plaguing a number of industrialized nations. Finally, some plants may also contribute to chemical weathering through acidic secretions. Whatever its cause, chemical weathering is a very slow process, but it is an important weathering process nonetheless.

PROCEDURE

1. Begin the activity by asking how many students have ever visited an old cemetery to just wander around and read the headstones. It's really fun to do, especially when the headstones are very old. Plus, cemeteries are great places to learn some geology!

2. Tell students that in the past in the United States, headstones were often made from limestone (or marble). (If you can obtain a good-sized piece of limestone, have it on hand to show students.) Explain that today, however, the inscriptions on most of those limestone/marble headstones have become faint and difficult to read, even on headstones only a hundred years old or less.

3. Now relate the fact that the ancient Egyptians, thousands of years ago, carved their inscriptions and art work into limestone. Their carvings, unlike those in the United States, are still clear, distinct, and easy to read to this day.

4. Ask students if they have any ideas as to why inscriptions made in limestone would fade after only a hundred years or so in the United States but remain virtually unchanged for thousands of years in Egypt. After students have made their suggestions, indicate that today's activity may provide some answers.

5. Group students and distribute the materials. Identify the gravel as being cleaned limestone and point out the container of vinegar.

6. Have each group use masking tape to label one cup Water and the other cup Vinegar. Students should the fill each cup about halfway with the indicated liquid. Make sure students note that both the water and the vinegar are clean and clear.

7. Instruct each group to drop half of the gravel pieces into the water and half into the vinegar and then carefully observe both cups for several minutes.

8. After five minutes or so, ask questions such as those that follow. (Note: the intensity of the vinegar/limestone reaction will depend upon the purity of the limestone.)

   - What is happening in each cup? (*A chemical reaction is occurring between the limestone and vinegar; nothing is happening in the water cup.*)

   - How do you know a chemical reaction is taking place between the limestone and the vinegar? (*The production of gas can be seen as tiny bubbles rising through the vinegar; also, if students listen closely, they may hear fizzing occurring in the cup containing vinegar.*)

   - Do you know what vinegar is, chemically? (*It is an acid, specifically acetic acid.*)

   - Is the limestone being decomposed (broken down) by the acid? (*yes*)

   - What do you think would eventually happen to the limestone if it were left in the acid long enough? (*It would completely decompose and disappear.*)

9. Inform students that the term *weathering* refers to the breakdown or decomposition of rock into smaller sizes. When decomposition is due to the rock being chemically changed, as students are presently observing, it is called chemical weathering (see Teacher Information).

10. Relate how precipitation is a naturally weak acid (see Teacher Information) which reacts with certain kinds of rocks, especially limestone, and causes chemical weathering. Ask students if they can now answer the question about the limestone inscriptions in Egypt versus those in the United States (step 4). (*The United States has a predominately humid climate in which acidic precipitation is common, thus there is lots of chemical weathering. Egypt has a desert climate in which there is little precipitation, thus minimal chemical weathering.*)

11. Have students leave the cups overnight. The next day, students will observe more evidence of chemical weathering in the vinegar cup. It should be somewhat cloudy and a tiny bit of residue from the decomposition of the limestone should be visible.

EXTENSIONS AND ADAPTATIONS

1. This activity is appropriate for use in a learning center.

2. Extend the activity as a class project. Every other day or so, replace the vinegar and the water in a setup with fresh fluids. If you continue this for several weeks to several months, the limestone pieces in the vinegar cup will dissolve to strikingly smaller sizes.

3. Leave a nongalvanized steel nail on an outside window sill for several days. Let students periodically observe the chemical weathering (rusting) that occurs.

4. Extend the discussion about rain being a naturally weak carbonic acid to include the issue of acid rain, which is plaguing a number of industrialized nations including the United States (see Teacher Information).

5. Take students on a field trip to a local cemetery if one is nearby and accessible. Let them relate inscription clarity to the composition and the age of the headstones.

6. Related activities Good-bye Rock—Shake, Rattle, and Roll on page 80, Groovy Glacier on page 83, Plant Power on page 86, and Ice Is Nice Unless You're a Rock on page 89.

BLOWING IN THE WIND _____

PRIMARY CONTENT
- Wind as an erosional agent
- Factors affecting wind erosion

PRIOR STUDENT KNOWLEDGE
The concept of weathering through completion of appropriate activities

PRE-ACTIVITY PREPARATION
1. Prepare 10 disposable aluminum pie pans as follows. For pans 1–6: fill to a depth of about 2.5 cm–5 cm (1 in.–2 in.) with topsoil and let the soil dry completely. For one of these pans, bow a 15 cm (6 in.) piece of thin cardboard and tape it around the inside rim; this will form a high barrier (see diagram in Procedure). For pan 7: fill to about 2.5 cm–5 cm (1 in.–2 in.) with topsoil but keep the soil moist by watering it as needed. For pan 8: fill to the same amount with sand. For pan 9: fill to the same amount with gravel. For pan 10: put in a section of grass-covered sod (dig it from the yard, for example), watering it as needed. You can obtain topsoil, sand, and gravel at any garden supply center.

2. Connect a long extension cord to an outside outlet or to an inside outlet with the cord extending outside through an open door or window.
3. Plan to do this activity on a nice day.

PROCESS SKILLS
Observing, comparing, inferring, hypothesizing, identifying variables, experimenting

GROUP SIZE
Class divided into 5 groups

MATERIALS PER GROUPS
- 10 disposable pie pans filled as directed (for whole class; see Pre-Activity Preparation)
- 1 variable-speed hair dryer (for whole class)
- 1 pair of safety goggles (for each group)
- 1 extension cord, 7.6 m to 30.5 m (25 ft to 100 ft) long, (for whole class)
- Paper towels for cleaning hands (for each group)

TEACHER INFORMATION

Weathering is the breakdown of rock into smaller pieces; erosion is the removal or transport of weathered material (sediment). As such, erosion is a process that wears down the earth's surface. Wind, water, gravity (landslides, for example), and glaciers are the primary agents of erosion. This activity focuses on wind. Wind energy is capable of moving vast amounts of material. Over long periods of time, wind can reshape a landscape.

As one might expect, the faster the wind speed, the greater the potential for wind erosion. This is because strong winds contain more energy and are thus able to carry more and larger-sized materials than can weaker winds. Windbreaks consisting of hedgerows or tree lines are frequently planted to help protect valuable farm land from erosion. Windbreaks work simply by slowing the speed of the wind. Wind erosion is typically greater over bare ground than over soil with a vegetative cover

(continues)

(continued)

because the roots of vegetation help anchor and hold soil particles in place. Wind erosion typically acts more on dry material than on moist material. The presence of water causes individual particles to clump together—in essence creating a larger (heavier) overall particle. The larger (heavier) the particle, the more difficult it is for wind to move it. In addition, moisture adds its own weight to material, which makes it more difficult for wind to move. This weight factor also explains why material with smaller-sized particles (even if the material is dry) is more subject to wind erosion than is material with larger-sized particles.

PROCEDURE

1. If necessary, review with students the concept of weathering and the production of sediment.

2. Introduce and define the term *erosion* (see Teacher Information). Be sure that students understand the distinction between weathering and erosion. Discuss the fact that there are four primary agents of erosion (carriers of sediment): wind, running water, gravity (landslides, for example), and glaciers.

3. Ask students to make some predictions concerning wind erosion. Below are five questions. Read the first question and have students make a prediction. Tally the predictions on the chalkboard and then have several students share the reasoning behind their predictions. Repeat the process for each of the remaining questions.

   Which material would be eroded the most by wind?
   a) dry material or moist material
   b) bare material or material covered by vegetation
   c) material composed of large-sized particles or material composed of smaller-sized particles
   d) material under gentle winds or material under strong winds
   e) material behind a line of shrubs or trees or material out in the open

4. Inform students that in today's activity they will be investigating the answer to each of these questions. Then divide the class into five groups.

5. Distribute a pan of dried topsoil to each of the five groups. Students should take turns rubbing the soil between their fingers to break up any clumps. They should work the entire mass of soil within the pans as thoroughly as possible.

6. Randomly distribute the remaining 5 pans, 1 pan to each group. Groups will end up with comparison pans as follows: dry soil/moist soil, dry soil/sod, dry soil/sand, dry soil/gravel, and dry soil/dry soil with a barrier. See illustration of a barrier pan.

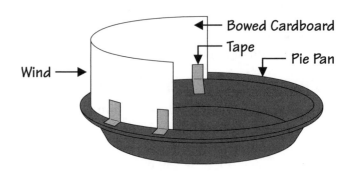

7. Take the groups (and the dryer and safety goggles) outside to an area within reach of the connected extension cord. Each group should bring along its 2 pans.

8. Demonstrate for students the procedure and the associated safety requirements for conducting the wind tests, as described in steps 9–10.

9. One student from each group will be the operator of the dryer (the Operator); the Operator must wear safety goggles. All other students must stand (upwind) behind the Operator and the setup to avoid the possibility of material blowing into their eyes.

10. The Operator should kneel down about 61 cm– 91 cm (2 ft–3 ft) from the pans (set side-by-side) and then lower the hair dryer close to the surface so that the wind will blow a little into, but mainly across, both pans simultaneously. (You might want to practice this once or twice yourself before the activity to establish the distance and angle of wind flow that produce the best results.) The Operator should set the dryer on high speed and turn it on. The Operator, and the rest of the group, should observe the results for a few seconds. The Operator should then set the dryer on low speed and turn it on to observe the effect of gentle winds. See the illustration at step 6 for the proper wind direction for the pan with the barrier.

11. Each group, one at a time, is to follow the above procedure to investigate wind action on their materials. You should have each group repeat the testing so that each student in the group gets a chance to be Operator.

12. As each group conducts its tests, it is important that the rest of the class also observe the results. Proper conclusions regarding wind erosion require the combined results of all the tests.

13. When the testing has been completed, return to the classroom to review and discuss results. This can be effectively done by repeating the questions from step 3 and asking students to give the reason behind each answer. Present explanations as needed (see Teacher Information).

EXTENSIONS AND ADAPTATIONS

1. Have students use appropriate sources to research sandstorms and dust storms, especially the factors that promote the occurrence of these events. Particularly relevant to this topic is the Dust Bowl region of the Central Plains of the United States in the mid 1930s.

2. Related activity Slowing It Down on page 99.

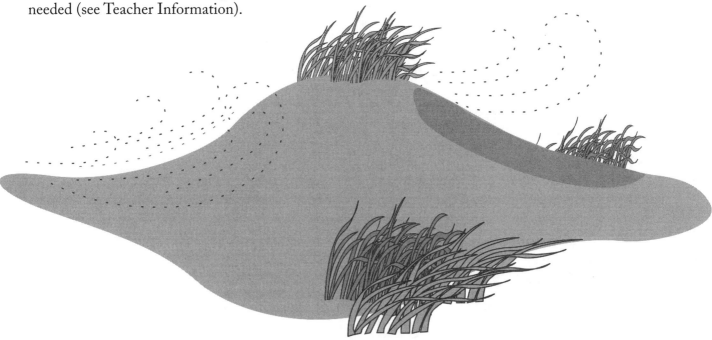

SLOWING IT DOWN

PRIMARY CONTENT
- Running water as an erosional agent
- Factors affecting water erosion

PRIOR STUDENT KNOWLEDGE
The concept of weathering through the completion of appropriate activities

PRE-ACTIVITY PREPARATION
1. Obtain a bag of topsoil from any garden supply center.
2. Each group will need a 3.79 L (1 gal) plastic milk jug (with cap). Ask students to bring these from home.
3. Collect various materials that students can use as ground covers (leaves, twigs, grass clippings, and mulch, for example). Put these materials in separate containers.

PROCESS SKILLS
Observing, comparing, inferring, recording data, communicating, hypothesizing, identifying variables, experimenting

GROUP SIZE
3–5 students

MATERIALS PER GROUP
- 1 plastic shoe box, cake pan, large disposable aluminum pie pan, or similar open-topped, watertight container of comparable size
- 1 drawing compass or nail (may be restricted to teacher use only; see note in Procedure step 4)
- 1 plastic milk jug with cap, 3.79 L (1 gal)
- 1 bag of topsoil (for whole class)
- 1 plastic cup to use as a scoop for the topsoil (for whole class)
- Available water (for whole class)
- Paper towels
- Scrap cardboard or poster board (for whole class)
- Scissors (for whole class)
- Containers of possible ground covers (for whole class; see Pre-Activity Preparation)
- 1 or more disposal buckets (for whole class)
- 1 sheet of paper
- 1 pencil

TEACHER INFORMATION

Weathering is the breakdown of rock into smaller pieces; erosion is the removal or transport of weathered material (sediment). As such, erosion is a process that wears down the earth's surface. Wind, water, gravity (landslides, for example), and glaciers are the primary agents of erosion. While there are several types of erosion related to water (erosion due

to groundwater, waves, and currents, for example), this activity focuses on one of the most powerful of all the erosional agents—the flow of water over the earth's surface, or running water. Running water can totally reshape a landscape in a comparatively short period of geological time.

(continues)

(continued)

A number of factors determine the amount of erosion that occurs due to running water. Three of the most important factors are the volume of water, the slope of the land, and the presence of or lack of vegetation cover. Water is the transporting vehicle of sediment. Thus, the greater the amount of water, the greater the amount of material that can be carried away. The slope of land determines the velocity of water flow and, thus, the amount of energy available to move material. Therefore, land in steeper slope is more subject to this type of erosion than is flatter land. Plant leaves and stems break the force of falling and running water. More importantly, plant roots anchor and hold material in place. Most attempts to control erosion involve a reduction in the amount of water flow (dams and water breaks), an increase in the holding capacity of soil (ground covers), and/or a reduction in the speed of water flow, either through obstacles (contour plowing, dams, and water breaks) or by reducing the angle of slope (terracing).

PROCEDURE

1. If necessary, review with students the concept of weathering and the production of sediment.

2. Introduce and define the term *erosion* (see Teacher Information). Be sure that students understand the distinction between weathering and erosion. Discuss the fact that there are four primary agents of erosion (carriers of sediment): wind, running water, gravity (landslides for example), and glaciers.

3. Tell students that today they will investigate erosion by running water, which accounts for more erosion of the earth's surface than any of the other agents.

4. Group students and distribute a container, a compass (or nail), and a plastic milk jug to each group. Each group's first task is to construct a water sprinkler by using a compass point or nail to poke holes in the upper part of the milk jug opposite the handle (see illustration). (Note: if student safety is in question, you should punch all the holes.)

Holes — Cap

Milk-Jug
Water
Sprinkler

5. Point out the bag of topsoil and instruct each group to fill its container to about one-third with soil. Students should also fill their sprinkler to about one-half with water.

6. Tell students to pretend that they are scientists who have been hired by the Hill Farmers Association of America. Farmers in this association are very concerned about erosion of their fields by running water. They want to know what factors affect the amount of erosion caused by running water, and they want to know what they can do to slow down the erosion of their hillside fields. You have divided yourselves into teams to investigate these questions by experimenting with water erosion on hill models.

7. Tell each group to use the soil to make the hill within their container. They should use the water sprinkler to create rain. If they need more soil for their hill, they should get it; if they have too much soil, they should return the excess. Students can do as many experiments as they like (build as many hills as they like on which to test erosion) by dumping the contents of their containers in the disposal buckets and building new hills. Caution students, however, not to let their containers get over half full of water before dumping.

8. Point out to each group the scissors, scrap cardboard or poster board, and containers of other materials (clippings and mulch, for example). Students may or may not decide to use these items and materials in their investigations.

9. Suggest that students in each group first talk things over and come up with a plan of attack rather than going about the investigation haphazardly. Also suggest that they record the results of their tests on a sheet of paper. Indicate that they can determine the amount of erosion by observing both the effects on the soil surface and the muddiness of the runoff.

10. Remind students that to conduct a fair comparison or test, everything should be kept the same expect the concept being tested (here, the relationship of running water and erosion). Review once more with students their two objectives as indicated in step 6.

11. Set the scientists to work. Give them plenty of time for experimentation. Circulate among the groups. Ask leading questions and provide hints and suggestions as needed.

12. When the groups have completed their investigations, have each group report their findings to the Hill Farmers Association of America (the class). Allow the farmers (the class) to question the scientists regarding their experimental methods and their results or conclusions. You be the moderator.

13. At the conclusion of the reports, summarize for students the major points realized through the experimentation. Present additional information about erosion by running water as you desire (see Teacher Information). Aspects and relationships typically discovered in this activity across all groups include these.

   • The greater the amount of flowing water, the greater the erosion, and vice versa.

   • The steeper the slope of the land, the greater the erosion, and vice versa.

   • The looser the soil, the greater the erosion, and vice versa.

   • The presence of a ground cover (vegetation in the natural environment) helps lessen erosion.

   • Different ground covers vary in their capacity to reduce erosion.

   • Contour plowing (making horizontal furrows with a pencil around the hill) reduces erosion; plowing up and down the hill vertically increases erosion.

   • The strategic location of dams or water breaks (cardboard sections, for example) reduces erosion.

   • Terracing the hillsides (by digging "steps" into the sides of the hill) reduces erosion.

EXTENSIONS AND ADAPTATIONS

1. Repeat the activity. This time let students investigate water erosion as it relates to different sizes of material—for example, fine soil versus sand versus gravel.

2. Have students research information on various erosion-reducing techniques used in agriculture—contour plowing and terrace farming, for example. Students can then present simple written or verbal reports.

3. Related activity Blowing in the Wind on page 95.

SETTLE DOWN!

PRIMARY CONTENT
- Sedimentation and the formation of sedimentary layers
- Differential settling rates of sediments of varying sizes

PRIOR STUDENT KNOWLEDGE

Concepts of weathering (the production of sediment) and erosion (the transport of sediment)

PRE-ACTIVITY PREPARATION

1. Cut the tops off four plastic milk jugs, 3.79 L (1 gal). Fill one of the jugs with topsoil, another with sand, another with small-sized gravel (pea gravel), and the last with medium-sized gravel. You can collect soil, sand, and gravel, or you can obtain them at any garden supply center.
2. Each student will need a tall, clear plastic bottle (with cap) with an opening somewhat larger than that of a 2 L soda bottle. The 1.89 L (64 oz) fruit juice bottles work well. Ask students to bring bottles from home.
3. Copy reproducible Sediment Drawing (page 105), one copy per student.

PROCESS SKILLS

Observing, comparing, inferring, hypothesizing

GROUP SIZE

Individual

MATERIALS PER GROUP
- 1 sheet of notebook paper
- Masking tape
- Scissors
- 1 tall, clear plastic bottle, with cap, as detailed in item 2 of the Pre-Activity Preparation
- Soil, sand, small-sized gravel, and medium-sized gravel in individual containers (for whole class; see Pre-Activity Preparation)
- 1 plastic cup, 355 L–473 mL (12 oz–16 oz), for transporting sediment
- Available water (for whole class)
- 1 copy of reproducible Sediment Drawing

TEACHER INFORMATION

Due to its energy of motion, flowing water (or air) has the capacity to carry or transport sediment—the faster the rate of flow, the greater the range of particle sizes that can be transported. When the speed of flow decreases, the sediment-carrying capacity of flowing water (such as a river) also decreases, and sediment must be deposited as a result. Step 10 in the Procedure lists some common reasons for reductions in river velocity. The depositing of sediments is referred to as sedimentation. While some sediment carried by rivers ends up being deposited in lakes or upon river flood plains, most of it is eventually carried to, and deposited in, oceans.

The natural result of material settling in a fluid (water or air) is the formation of sediment layers. If the carrying capacity of flowing water (a river) at the time of speed reduction were low, the water would be transporting only small-sized materials. In this case, there would not be much difference in particle sizes among the layers. On the other hand, if the carrying capacity of the river were high, the river would be carrying materials of many different sizes. In this case (and as modeled in this activity), the sediment layers would show distinct differences in material sizes—with the largest size forming the bottom layer and the smallest size forming the top layer. This separation of sediment sizes, called sorting, is due simply to the fact that larger (heavier) particles settle faster than smaller (lighter) particles. It is through the sedimentation process that sedimentary rocks (layered rocks) eventually form.

PROCEDURE

1. If necessary, review with students the fact that the physical and chemical weathering of rock produces smaller-sized rock particles called sediment. These unconsolidated particles are then carried away (transported) by agents of erosion, especially running water and wind.

2. Ask students, "What happens to this sediment? Is it just carried around forever, or does it end up somewhere? If it ends up somewhere, where might that be?"

3. After students have expressed their ideas, discuss with them the definition of *sedimentation*—"the dropping or deposition of sediments by their erosional agents." Then talk about likely sites of sedimentation (see Teacher Information).

4. Inform students that while wind deposits and glacial deposits are significant, they are not nearly as plentiful and important as water deposits of sediment. In today's activity, students will investigate what happens to sediment when it is deposited by water (settles out in water).

5. Distribute materials to each student.

6. A wide-outlet funnel makes putting sediment into the bottles much easier. Therefore, first show students how to roll a sheet of paper into a cone (funnel) shape, taping to secure. After students have done this, have them cut the bottom of the cone off, giving it a wide outlet—but still narrow enough to just fit into the opening of the tall container.

7. Point out the 4 containers of different-sized sediments. Have each student make a single trip to the containers, putting a handful of material from each container into his/her transport cup. Each student should take the cup, with its 4 sizes of sediment, and then pour the sediment into his/her bottle with the aid of the funnel. Have students temporarily pair up to do the pouring. One can hold the funnel in place while the other pours.

8. Now instruct each student to fill the bottle to about four-fifths with water and then cap the bottle tightly. Ask students questions such as:
   - What might the materials and water in the bottle represent? (*sediments in a river*)
   - Isn't the water in a river flowing? (*yes*)
   - Then shouldn't we put the water in our models in motion as well? (*yes*)

9. Have students put their water in motion by repeatedly turning the bottles upside-down, then right-side-up. As they continue the motion, ask questions such as:
   - Why aren't the sediments lying on the bottom of the bottle anymore? Why are they now mixing throughout the water (being suspended in the water)? (*Because the water is in motion, it has enough energy to pick up and carry [keep suspended] the particles.*)
   - Are the different sizes of the sediments mixing or are they staying grouped together? (*They are mixing because all of them are in movement in the water.*)

10. As students continue the mixing motion, indicate that the speed at which their waters are flowing is going to decrease. In nature, this might be caused by a river entering a standing body of water such as a lake or the ocean; or it might be due to a mountain stream coming onto flatland; or it could be caused by a river flooding, with that part of the river that is out of its banks (out of the channel) decreasing greatly in speed.

(continues)

(continued)

11. To model a decrease in flow rate, instruct students to stop the mixing, stand their bottles upright, and observe what happens to the sediments over a period of five minutes or so. Then have students each draw on the reproducible what their sediments look like. Assist students with reading the directions as necessary.

12. After students have completed their drawings, discuss the results through questions such as those that follow, presenting explanations as necessary. (See Answer Key on page 154.)

    • What happened to the sediments when the water motion slowed and stopped? Why? *(The sediments settled to the bottom of the bottle because the slower moving water did not have enough energy to keep them suspended.)*

    • Did you notice anything about the pattern in which the materials settled? *(The sediment settled out in distinct layers, and the layers were arranged according to particle size: the larger gravel on the bottom, then the smaller gravel, then the sand, and then a soil layer at the very top. Some of the sediment remained suspended in the water as indicated by the water's dirty appearance.)*

    • Why did the sediments settle in layers, why was there a separation in sizes, and why were the largest particles on bottom and the smallest on top? (see Teacher Information)

13. Discuss how layering is a major characteristic of water-deposited sediments and, to a lesser extent, of wind-deposited materials. Introduce the concept of sedimentary rocks by asking students if they have ever seen layers of rock in road cuts and if they think that the original material that formed those rocks was deposited. *(Layered rock indicates that the material forming the rock was originally sediment which was deposited in water or sometimes by wind).*

EXTENSIONS AND ADAPTATIONS

1. This activity is appropriate for use in a learning center.

2. Allow the bottles to sit undisturbed overnight. Additional layers of very fine material will settle out and form new layers.

3. If possible, take students on a field trip to a road cut displaying layered sedimentary rock. If this is not feasible, show them pictures, slides, or a video displaying layered rock.

4. Related activity Instant Rocks on page 111.

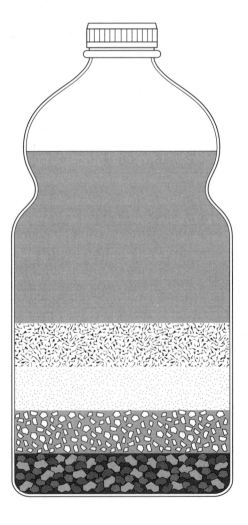

Earth Science Activities (KSAM)

SETTLE DOWN! _____

SEDIMENT DRAWING

Name_____

Directions: Wait about five minutes after you stop the water motion in your bottle. Then use the outline below to draw in what the sediments in your bottle look like. Also draw in the water level.

ROCK CRITTER _____

PRIMARY CONTENT
Developing and interpreting classifications

PRIOR STUDENT KNOWLEDGE
No special prior knowledge is required.

PRE-ACTIVITY PREPARATION
1. Each student will need 1 rock, fist-sized or a little larger. The type, shape, and color of the rocks are not important. You can collect rocks, or you can ask students to bring rocks to school.

2. Assemble a variety of materials that students can use to make a rock critter, for example: scissors, construction paper, glue, paints, brushes, markers, cotton balls, glue-on eyes, colored pipe cleaners (the fuzzy kind used for crafts), string, colored feathers, rubber bands, and so on. Most of these, plus many other items, are available at hobby and craft supply stores.

PROCESS SKILLS
Observing, comparing, classifying, inferring, communicating

GROUP SIZE
Individual, followed by groups of 5–7 students

MATERIALS PER GROUP
- 1 rock, fist-sized or slightly larger, for each student
- Availability to each student of a variety of materials and supplies for decorating rocks, as detailed in the Pre-Activity Preparation
- 2 sheets of plain paper (for each group)
- 1 sheet of plain paper for each student

TEACHER INFORMATION

This is a fun activity for students at the 2–3 level. The activity is used primarily as an introduction or starter activity for a unit on rocks and is designed to put rocks into students' hands for reasons other than throwing! It also serves to reacquaint students with both developing and interpreting classifications—an important skill in working with rocks in other activities.

PROCEDURE

1. Tell students that today they will be doing a rather unusual science activity—each of them will create a rock critter!

2. Distribute a rock to each student and point out the variety of materials and supplies available to them. Inform students that they do not have to use all the available items; they can pick and choose as they wish.

3. Tell students that they each are to create a rock critter. The critters can look like whatever students want them to look like; the only limitation is their imagination. From the available materials, students can draw, paint, and glue their critters into creation.

4. Set students to work. Provide them with ample time to make their critters.

5. After students have finished and all the glue on the critters has dried, divide students into groups of 5–7. Each student is to have his/her rock critter. Distribute 2 sheets of paper to each group and 1 sheet to each student. Assign each group an identification letter (group A, group B, and so on). Each group is to record its identification letter on one sheet of paper and display it in a visible location.

6. Each group is then to independently come up with a criterion by which to classify its critters into two categories. A few of many possibilities include: tails/no tails, feet/no feet, 2 feet/4 feet, antennae/no antennae, feather(s)/no feathers, 1 eye/2 eyes, and fur (cotton)/no fur. Each group should record its selected criterion along with its identification letter on the second sheet of paper and give it to you.

7. Now have each group use the criterion to sort its critters into two categories. Check the work of each group to be sure that all critters are correctly classified according to the recorded criterion.

8. Leaving the group critters assembled in their categories, students are to individually rotate with pencil and paper among all the groups' work stations. At each station, each student is to study the groupings and make a guess as to the criterion used to categorize the critters. The student should record on paper the group's identification letter and his/her guess. Two to four minutes per station is usually ample time.

9. When all students have finished, review the results group by group. For example, ask several students not in group A to read their guesses as to how group A's critters were classified. Then read to the class the actual classification criterion as recorded by group A. Repeat the process with group B, C, and so on. Have each student keep track of how many classifications he/she guessed correctly.

10. Discuss why some classifications may have been more difficult to interpret than others.

EXTENSIONS AND ADAPTATIONS

1. That portion of this activity in which the rock critters are created is appropriate for use in a learning center.

2. Have students write a creative story about their rock critters.

3. Let students present to the class a verbal summary of the characteristics of their rock critters—what they eat, where they're from, what their habitat is like, and so on.

4. Let the class build a rock critter zoo.

5. Display the rock critters around the room and invite other classes in to see them.

6. Related activities All Rocks Are Not Created Equal on page 108 and Instant Rocks on page 111.

ALL ROCKS ARE NOT CREATED EQUAL _____

PRIMARY CONTENT
Ranking rocks according to various physical properties

PRIOR STUDENT KNOWLEDGE
Basic exposure to the concept of minerals

PRE-ACTIVITY PREPARATION
Each group will need a bag or box containing a variety of different rocks—the greater the diversity in rock types, sizes, shapes, and appearances, the better. The rock sets for each group need not be identical. You can obtain rocks in a variety of ways: you can collect them, you can purchase them from educational supply companies, you can ask students to bring rocks to class, you can send letters home asking parents for rock donations, or you can borrow rocks from colleagues. Also, many states have a Geological Survey or Department of Natural Resources that supply rock sets to teachers at minimal cost (sometimes free).

PROCESS SKILLS
Observing, comparing, classifying

GROUP SIZE
2–3 students

MATERIALS PER GROUP
- 1 prepared bag or box containing a variety of different rocks (see Pre-Activity Preparation)
- 1 hand lens (or more if possible)
- (Optional) Laboratory scale or balance (for whole class)

TEACHER INFORMATION

As the primary constituent of the earth, rocks provide geologists with valuable information. Rocks can be described and classified by their physical properties. Being able to observe characteristics and then use them to make logical classifications is fundamental not only in the earth sciences, but in all the sciences. In selecting characteristics by which to describe or classify materials, some choices are more useful than others. Characteristics based on physical properties are more useful than characteristics based solely, or partly, on personal opinion and preference because comparisons about the latter can vary so much from person to person (for example, what is beautiful to

one may not be beautiful to another). You should, therefore, encourage students to utilize objective criteria that are based on definite physical properties (size, weight, color, and so on). Even some physical properties call for some personal judgment—what is heavy to one may seem light to another, for example. It is for this reason that you should have students use quantitative criteria whenever possible. That way, for example, if a property of weight is stated as 500 grams and above/below 500 grams instead of heavy/light, there will be no problem with interpretation. Good classifications are important because they help people organize materials for easier and more effective study. Classifications are also critical in the identification of materials—rocks, for example.

PROCEDURE

1. Open the activity by asking two students of the same sex to come to the front of the room. Ask the class to describe, in as much detail as possible, how the two are different and how they are similar, based on their physical characteristics. Stress that students may only use physical (observable and/or measurable) attributes for comparisons. Saying that student A is funny and student B is not funny does not qualify as a physical characteristic, for example. (Note: make your student selections with care. Do not select students who might be sensitive about any physical traits—height or weight, for example.)

2. After the class has made the comparison, lead student to understand that although the two students are similar in many ways, there are enough physical differences between the two that they can be individually recognized.

3. Then point out to the class that many people have never really taken a close look at rocks—to many, all rocks are basically alike, a rock is a rock. This means that these people have only observed the similarities among rocks and have not looked closely enough or long enough to see the differences. Explain that rocks, just like people, have physical characteristics that make them different from one another and that rocks can be classified according to those characteristics.

4. Tell students that in today's activity they will be taking a close look at rocks in an attempt to observe similarities and differences among them.

5. Group students and distribute the materials. Direct each group to place its rocks on a desk.

6. Give the students in each group time to observe their rocks. Encourage them to use their direct senses—to look at the rocks closely and unhurriedly, to feel them, to smell them. They should also look at the rocks through the hand lens.

7. After allowing adequate time for observation, have groups rank-order their rocks based on size, from smallest to largest. Each group must reach a decision as to the ranking. After groups have completed the rankings, ask if there were any disagreements within groups as to how any rocks should be ranked. If there were, ask the disagreeing parties to state their cases. Then find out how the group made its final decision.

8. Repeat step 7, in turn, for each of the following characteristics:
   - color or shade (from the darkest to the lightest)
   - importance (from the least important to the most important)
   - feel (from the roughest to the smoothest)
   - beauty (from the prettiest to the ugliest)
   - weight (from the lightest to the heaviest) (weight can be estimated by feel or, if available, rocks can be weighed on a scale or balance)

9. Review results with the class. Point out that the following characteristics (usually) resulted in fewer disagreements than others: size, color or shade, feel, and weight. These characteristics are based on physical properties—attributes which are directly observable, measurable, or testable. As such, their meanings are more definite and universal. Yet, the meanings of some of these characteristics (feel and estimated weight) call for more personal judgment than the meanings of other characteristics (size, measured weight, and color).

10. Also point out that the following characteristics (usually) generated more controversy and disagreements than others: importance and beauty. These characteristics are not based on physical properties. The meanings of these characteristics are variable because the determinations of those meanings rely heavily on individual preferences or opinions.

11. Tell students that they have been classifying rocks and that classifying is an important skill in geology. Since most of the earth is made of rock, rocks provide valuable information about the earth. To study rocks, geologists must be able to identify them. That means that rocks must first be classified in various ways. Therefore, good classifications are very important. Lead students to the conclusion that good, workable classifications must be based on physical characteristics, not on nonphysical attributes.

EXTENSIONS AND ADAPTATIONS

1. In Procedure step 8, let students add additional criteria for rank-ordering the rocks.

2. Related activities Rock Critter on page 106 and Instant Rocks on page 111.

INSTANT ROCKS _____

PRIMARY CONTENT

- Introducing sedimentary rocks
- Understanding methods of sediment lithification
- Creating sedimentary rocks in the classroom

PRIOR STUDENT KNOWLEDGE

The concepts of sediments, sedimentation, and the formation of sedimentary layers; suggested completion of the activity Settle Down! on page 102

PRE-ACTIVITY PREPARATION

1. Collect or purchase (at most garden centers) medium-sized gravel and clay-rich soil (topsoil, for example), enough to supply each group with 118 mL ($\frac{1}{2}$ c) of each.
2. Obtain a small bag of mortar mix (not concrete mix) at a building supply center.
3. If possible, obtain one or more samples of conglomerate and shale. If necessary, borrow them from the junior high school or senior high school earth science teacher.

PROCESS SKILLS

Observing, comparing, inferring

GROUP SIZE

2–4 students

MATERIALS PER GROUP

- 1 plastic foam cup with about 118 mL ($\frac{1}{2}$ c) of medium gravel
- 1 section of heavy cardboard measuring roughly 15 cm x 15 cm (6 in. x 6 in.)
- 1 marking pen
- 1 bag of mortar mix (for teacher use)
- 1 pail, 3.79 L (1 gal), for mixing mortar (for teacher use)
- Available water (for whole class)
- 1 measuring cup (for whole class)
- 1 mixing spoon or paint stirrer (for teacher use)
- 1 whipped topping container (or similar container) with about 118 mL ($\frac{1}{2}$ c) of clay-rich soil
- 1 plastic cup (any size) for transporting water
- 2 sheets of aluminum foil, each roughly 30.5 cm (1 ft) square
- 2 or 3 books
- Paper towels for cleaning hands
- Desktop surface
- 1 sheet of newspaper for covering desk
- Display sample(s) of conglomerate and shale (for whole class)

TEACHER INFORMATION

The conversion of loose, unconsolidated sediment into sedimentary rock is called lithification. Through lithification, separate particles are combined into a solid mass—a sedimentary rock. There are two primary types of lithification. One type occurs through the cementation of particles by natural cements within the water into which the sediments have been deposited. These cements can be suspended in the water (most commonly, muds) or dissolved in the water. Either way, the cement fills the pores between the grains and holds them together. The second type of lithification occurs through compaction—much in the same way that loose snowflakes are compacted into a snowball. This process operates most efficiently on wet, small-sized sediments. The weight of overlying layers of sediment obviously plays a critical role in compaction.

PROCEDURE

1. If necessary, review with students the concepts of sediments and sediment deposition and the formation of sediment layers.

2. Inform students that when many layers of sediment have accumulated, those at the bottom of the sequence become converted into layers of solid rock. Ask students if they have ever seen layers of rock in road cuts. Indicate that rocks that have been formed by the conversion of sediment into a solid mass are called sedimentary rocks.

3. Ask students if they have any ideas as to how sediment is converted from loose, unconsolidated pieces into solid rock. What makes the individual particles stick or stay together? Allow students to present their ideas but do not provide content information at this time.

4. As you divide students into groups, tell them that in today's activity they will see two ways in which sedimentary rocks can form. Students will also create their own rocks in the process!

Part One: Making Conglomerate— Lithification by Cementation

1. Provide each group with a plastic foam cup containing gravel, a cardboard section, and a marking pen. Have the students in each group mark their initials on their cups. Ask students what they think the gravel represents. *(deposited sediment)*

2. Tell students that when water seeps and percolates through deposited sediments, the water often has dissolved or suspended in it materials that can act as natural cements. There are many such materials, ranging from muds to various dissolved minerals. Thus, the water in which the sediments are deposited frequently plays the role of a cementing solution.

3. Inform students that you will now prepare a cementing solution to represent the kind of cementing solution that might be found in the natural environment. Prepare a thin, soupy mortar solution as follows: measure out 2.1 L (70 oz) of mortar mix and put it in a pail. Add 590 mL (20 oz) of water. Mix well by stirring. This will yield enough cementing solution for 15 groups.

4. Instruct each group to bring its cup (with gravel) to the cementing solution. Have students measure out 118 mL (4 oz) of the solution and pour it into the cup. (You should mix the mortar mix between each pouring.)

5. After the cementing solution has been added to the gravel, each group should hold the cardboard section tightly over the mouth of the cup and shake it for about thirty seconds.

6. Each group should then discard the cardboard sections and place the cup in a place where it can remain undisturbed until the next day.

Part Two: Making Shale— Lithification by Compaction

1. Provide each group with a container of soil, a marking pen, a plastic cup, 2 sheets of foil, paper towels, and 2 or 3 books to serve as weights.

2. Ask students what they think the soil represents. *(deposited sediments of a size much smaller than the gravel)* Tell students that sometimes, if sediment size is small enough, the sediment may be converted to rock in another way.

3. Instruct each group to fill the plastic cup to about one-half with water.

4. Students should slowly add water to the soil, mixing the soil and water with their fingers. They should add only enough water to give the mixture a consistency of very thick pudding (it should not be watery). Students ought to be able to pick the mass up and form it into a pliable mud ball.

5. Have students wash and dry their hands.

6. Students in each group are to place a sheet of aluminum foil flat on a desk and then mark their initials in one corner. They should then place the mud ball in the center of the foil sheet, place the other foil sheet over the ball, and place books on top of the second sheet. They can add extra pressure by pushing down on the top book. Ask questions such as:

   - What are the books (with help from you) doing to the sediment? *(Their weight is pressing down on the sediment, causing it to squeeze and compact.)*

   - What do the extra books represent? *(additional layers of sediment)*

7. Tell students that they do not have as much time as nature does. Therefore, to help the drying process, have students remove the upper layers of sediment (the books) and the top sheet of foil. They should leave the pancake-shaped mud to dry overnight.

Part Three: Seeing Results

1. The next day, distribute newspaper to each group for use as a desk covering.

2. Have each group retrieve its mud sample. Ask students to describe the results. *(The originally loose sediment [soil] is now a hard, solid mass.)*

3. Show students the sample(s) of shale. Have them note the similarities between their samples and the shale. *(flattened and sheetlike, hard, muddy color)* Inform them that these samples of shale rock formed in much the same way as their samples formed. Ask through what process the soil particles are now being held together in the shale or in their samples. *(through wetting and compaction followed by drying)*

4. Now have each group retrieve its plastic foam cup and tear the foam away from the rock inside. Tell students to break their sample into 3 or 4 pieces. (The broken pieces will look more rocklike than the cup-shaped original.) Ask students to describe the results. *(The loose sediment [gravel] is now a hard, solid mass—very similar to an actual rock.)*

5. Show students the sample(s) of conglomerate. Have them note the similarities between their samples and the conglomerate. *(large, easily visible rock particles held together by a very fine material— a cement)*

EXTENSIONS AND ADAPTATIONS

1. Show students samples of sandstone, another sedimentary rock that is held together by cementation.

2. If available, take students on a field trip to a road cut displaying layered sedimentary rock. If this is not feasible, show them pictures, slides, or a video displaying layered rock. Ask students to infer the ancient environment that existed when the deposits forming the sedimentary rock layers were deposited. *(The area must have been a water environment [commonly ocean] into which the sediments were deposited.)*

3. You can use plaster of Paris mixed to a very thin consistency instead of mortar in this activity. The result, however, does not look as realistic as that formed with mortar.

4. Try making sandstone through cementation resulting from the precipitation of dissolved minerals in water. Cover 118 mL ($\frac{1}{2}$ c) of fine sand with a saturated solution of Epsom salts and then wait until it completely evaporates. (Make the solution by dissolving Epsom salts in warm water until no more salt will go into solution.)

5. Related activities Settle Down! on page 102, Rock Critter on page 106, and All Rocks Are Not Created Equal on page 108.

MAN OH MAN, DIG THEM BONES! _____

PRIMARY CONTENT

• Introducing dinosaurs
• Understanding the nature of dinosaur finds and dinosaur skeletons

PRIOR STUDENT KNOWLEDGE

The basic concept of fossils

PRE-ACTIVITY PREPARATION

Copy reproducible Dinosaur Picture Sheet (page 116), one copy per student, and reproducible Scattered Skeleton Scene (page 117), two copies per student.

PROCESS SKILLS

Observing, comparing, classifying, inferring, predicting, communicating

GROUP SIZE

Individual

MATERIALS PER GROUP

• 1 copy of reproducible Dinosaur Picture Sheet
• Crayons
• 2 copies of reproducible Scattered Skeleton Scene
• Scissors
• Glue
• 1 sheet of unlined white paper

TEACHER INFORMATION

The dinosaurs were reptiles that lived during the Mesozoic era some 230 million to 65 million years ago. Dinosaurs were primarily land-dwelling animals. They ranged in size from smaller-than-a-chicken to mammoth—up to 30.5 m (100 ft) long, 18.3 m (60 ft) tall, and 150 tons in weight.

While it is still assumed that many dinosaurs were cold-blooded, evidence suggests that at least some dinosaurs, unlike present-day reptiles, were warm-blooded and much more closely related to birds than had been previously thought. Whether all dinosaurs were cold-blooded or some were warm-blooded is still a major topic of debate and study within the science of vertebrate paleontology.

Dinosaurs became extinct some 65 million years ago—about 60 million years before humans came onto the scene! Why dinosaurs died out is still not known with certainty. Since human beings have never seen a whole dinosaur, alive or dead (soft tissue decomposes too rapidly to be preserved), what we know about dinosaurs comes mainly from the study of their hard parts (bones and teeth)—parts that can be preserved as fossils. We can, therefore, only infer how dinosaurs looked when they were alive.

PROCEDURE

1. Introduce the activity by discussing with students some general aspects about dinosaurs—what they were, when they lived, and how big they were, for example (see Teacher Information).

2. To supplement the discussion, distribute the reproducible Dinosaur Picture Sheet to each student. It shows what paleontologists think that six of the most common dinosaurs looked like and what their relative sizes were as compared to the size of a typical elementary school student.

3. Ask students what they think dinosaurs look like when paleontologists find them. Do the scientists find whole animals, flesh and all? Do they find the animals' skeletons intact and connected like the skeletons seen in a museum?

4. Lead students to understand that: (a) dinosaur finds consist of preserved bones and teeth (the hard parts) of the animals because flesh decomposes too quickly to become fossilized; (b) the bones are not in whole connected skeletons because ligaments— the tissues that hold the bones together—also quickly rot; (c) because bones are often moved by erosional agents, especially running water, the skeleton of a dinosaur may be spread over a large area; and (d) fossilized dinosaur bones are those that become buried in sediment which eventually hardens to solid rock due to the pressure of new layers of sediment above; thus, dinosaur bones are found embedded in rock layers.

5. Distribute crayons and one copy of Scattered Skeleton Scene to each student. The reproducible is an illustration of a cross section showing dinosaur bones buried in rock layers beneath the present surface. Review the cross section with students and show them how it illustrates the four aspects discussed in step 4.

6. Have students color the picture. Encourage them to add surface details such as present-day houses, trees, the sun, clouds, and so on.

7. Now have students become official paleontologists and dig up the dinosaur bones so that they can be reconstructed into a complete skeleton. So that students do not have to destroy their colored pictures, distribute a second copy of Scattered Skeleton Scene to each student along with glue, scissors, and a sheet of unlined white paper.

8. Instruct students to cut out the skeleton sections on the second copy by cutting just *inside* the dotted lines. They should then glue the sections together on the white paper to form a whole skeleton. See Answer Key on page 154 for a picture of the completed skeleton.

9. Let students each draw and color a museum scene around the completed dinosaur skeleton.

10. On the wall or bulletin board, display students' pictures of the buried dinosaur bones and the completed skeleton.

EXTENSIONS AND ADAPTATIONS

1. This activity is appropriate for use in a learning center.

2. Related activities My Dinosaur Name Is . . . on page 118, Dinosaur Diorama on page 120, and Mystery Footprints on page 122.

MAN OH MAN, DIG THEM BONES! _____

DINOSAUR PICTURE SHEET

Name_____

Tyrannosaurus

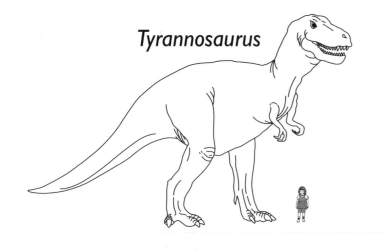

Corythosaurus

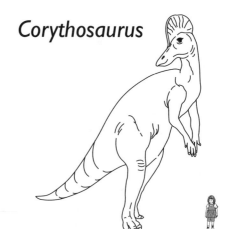

Pinacosaurus

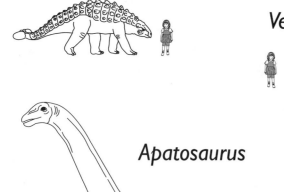

Velociraptor

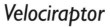

Pentaceratops

Apatosaurus

©Curriculum Associates, Inc.   *Earth Science Activities (KSAM)*

MAN OH MAN, DIG THEM BONES! _____

SCATTERED SKELETON SCENE

Name_____

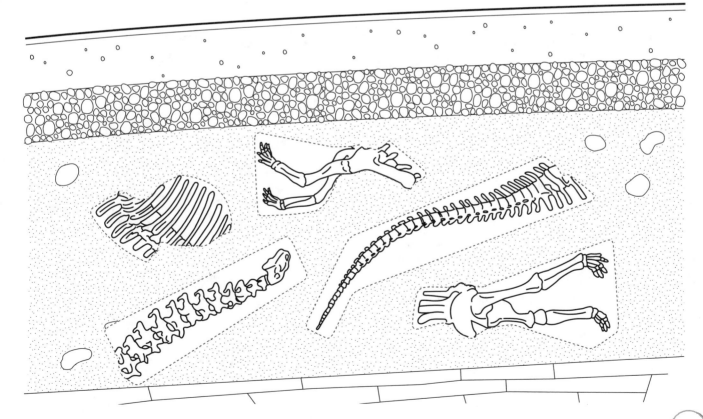

MY DINOSAUR NAME IS ... _____

PRIMARY CONTENT
- Reconstructing a dinosaur skeleton
- Understanding the nature of dinosaur finds

PRIOR STUDENT KNOWLEDGE
Suggested completion of the activity Man Oh Man, Dig Them Bones! on page 114

PRE-ACTIVITY PREPARATION
To make a dinosaur-find bag for each student, put in a plastic sandwich bag 6 pipe cleaners of the following lengths: 2 whole, 4 halves, and 8 fourths. Also prepare a bone-bank bag for the class. This bag should consist of extra pipe cleaners of various lengths. Cutting the pipe cleaners is a snap if you use a paper cutter; the pipe cleaners cut easily and you can cut several simultaneously. With a little extra labor, you can also cut the pipe cleaners with wire cutters.

PROCESS SKILLS
Inferring, communicating

GROUP SIZE
Individual

MATERIALS PER GROUP
- 1 prepared dinosaur-find bag (see Pre-Activity Preparation)
- 1 copy of reproducible Dinosaur Picture Sheet that was used in the activity Man Oh Man, Dig Them Bones! on page 114 (alert students ahead of time that they will need this reproducible and they should have it on hand for this activity)
- 1 prepared bone-bank bag (for whole class; see Pre-Activity Preparation)

TEACHER INFORMATION

Although all the information that students need is provided in the activity Procedure, you might note that the bone-bank process is similar to what vertebrate paleontologists do. The "missing bones" problem is very prevalent; very few digs are ever complete in terms of the skeletons obtained. Usually, however, enough bones are found for the paleontologist to know which bones are missing and their approximate size and shape. In order to have a complete skeleton for study and observation, the missing bones are often reconstructed using plaster. That way, for example, when we see *Tyrannosaurus Rex* in a museum, we see it standing on two legs instead of only on the one leg that was found!

PROCEDURE

1. If necessary, review with students the characteristics of dinosaur finds and dinosaur fossils that they learned about in the activity Man Oh Man, Dig Them Bones! on page 114 (see Procedure step 4 in that activity).

2. Tell the class that the information in the activity Man Oh Man, Dig Them Bones! is an introduction and thus is simplified. In reality, dinosaur finds are a little more complex than what was depicted in that activity. Specifically:

   a) Dinosaur skeletons are not found in just five or six separated sections, with the bones in each section already connected. Rather, none of the dinosaur bones are connected; they are all separated, scattered, and mixed. Ask students if they know why. (*All the ligaments would have rotted, causing all the bones to separate.*)

   b) Usually, not all of the bones of a dinosaur are present in the find; some bones will be missing. Ask students why. (*Some may have been carried off by other animals soon after the death of the dinosaur; some may not have been buried quickly enough to be preserved and fossilized; and, most importantly, some may have been removed by erosion.*)

   c) Sometimes there are too many bones in a dig for a single skeleton. Ask students why. (*Several different animals may have all died at the same location.*)

3. Explain to students that it is the job of a paleontologist to figure out which bones belong to a skeleton and which don't, where the different bones go in a skeleton, and whether any bones are missing.

4. Tell students that they are each now official paleontologists. Each of them has come across a new dinosaur find.

5. Distribute a dinosaur-find bag to each student. Have students note that their finds consist of a variety of bones (pipe cleaners of different lengths). The bones are all separate, and they are all mixed-up.

6. Inform students that it is their job to each build a dinosaur skeleton from the bones in their finds by bending the bones to desired shapes and by attaching the bones to one another by bending or twisting. Some students may find that they do not need all the bones in their finds. They may have "extra" bones from other animals. Other students, however, may not have enough bones to complete their skeletons. They may have bones missing as a result of erosion.

7. To any student paleontologists plagued by missing bones, explain that a bone bank is available at the front of the room. The bone bank contains a quantity of bones of various lengths which students can use if they need them to complete a skeleton.

8. Tell students that they may construct a skeleton modeled after an actual dinosaur, using the Dinosaur Picture Sheet as a reference. Or, they can build a previously undiscovered dinosaur (an imaginary dinosaur of their choice). Regardless, students must give their dinosaurs names, either real or made-up.

9. Set students to work. Assist them with the bending of small pieces of pipe cleaner if necessary.

10. When the skeletons are completed, have a show-and-tell session during which each student can identify and display his/her dinosaur to the class.

EXTENSIONS AND ADAPTATIONS

1. This activity is appropriate for use in a learning center.

2. Have students each draw a picture of what their dinosaur looked like when it was alive.

3. Have students each write a story about their dinosaur—where it lived, what it ate, how it died, and so on.

4. If actual dinosaurs are modeled, have those students find out as much information as they can about those dinosaurs.

5. Make modeling-clay or papier-mâché models of dinosaurs.

6. Related activities Dinosaur Diorama on page 120 and Mystery Footprints on page 122.

DINOSAUR DIORAMA _____

PRIMARY CONTENT

Constructing a three-dimensional prehistoric scene

PRIOR STUDENT KNOWLEDGE

Introduction to dinosaurs; suggested completion of activity Man Oh Man, Dig Them Bones! on page 114

PRE-ACTIVITY PREPARATION

1. Each group will need a shoe box. Ask student to bring these from home.
2. Each group will need several small dinosaur models. Sources include educational supply companies, toy stores, science and nature stores, and gift shops at science centers and museums. Since dinosaur models are common toys, you may wish to ask students to bring them from home (labeled with the owners' initials so that they can be returned after the activity).
3. Assemble a variety of materials that students can use in fashioning their dioramas. Materials might include: tape, construction paper, glue, paints, brushes, markers, crayons, rocks (for boulders), gravel (for smaller rocks), soil, sand, grass clippings (for ground cover), small clumps of grass (for bushes), evergreen sprigs and twigs (for trees and vegetation), and modeling clay (for bases to hold up the trees).
4. Assemble resource materials on dinosaurs.

PROCESS SKILLS

Inferring, communicating

GROUP SIZE

1–3 students

MATERIALS PER GROUP

- 1 shoe box (lid not necessary)
- Several small dinosaur models
- Scissors
- An assortment of materials and supplies for fashioning the dioramas (for whole class; see Pre-Activity Preparation)
- Resource materials on dinosaurs (for whole class)

TEACHER INFORMATION

This is a high-interest activity that students enjoy. It also promotes additional learning about dinosaurs and their habitats through the use of resource materials.

The activity is very versatile. It can be used near the beginning of a dinosaur unit to build interest and promote independent study. It can also be used as a capstone activity for a dinosaur unit, in which students can demonstrate what they have learned.

PROCEDURE

1. Ask how many students have ever been to museums or science centers and observed lifelike scenes with realistic models and landscapes. Indicated that these are called dioramas. Let those students who have seen dioramas share their experiences with the rest of the class.

2. Ask students why they think that dioramas tend to be so interesting and attract so much attention. *(Since they are three-dimensional, to scale, and include accompanying scenery, dioramas are much more lifelike and realistic than two-dimensional representations.)*

3. Tell students that today you would like them to make dinosaur dioramas.

4. Group students and distribute the materials. Point out the availability of assorted materials for fashioning the dioramas and the availability of resource materials for looking up additional information about dinosaurs and their habitats.

5. First have each group cut away one of the long sides of the shoe box (assist if necessary), resulting in a three-sided box with two ends and a back.

6. Each group is to begin work on a diorama. Tell students that this is a project that can span several days if necessary; therefore, they should put thought and planning into the design of their diorama and work carefully to create the best and most realistic diorama possible.

7. Assist groups as necessary by providing construction and decoration ideas and/or by helping them with the actual construction. See illustration for an example of a completed diorama.

8. After groups have completed their dioramas (again, they need not be completed in one day), have each group write a description of its diorama—the animals, the scenery, what's going on at the instant in time portrayed by the diorama, and so on.

9. Conduct a show-and-tell session during which each group displays and describes its diorama to the class.

EXTENSIONS AND ADAPTATIONS

1. This activity is appropriate for use as a learning center.

2. Display the dioramas and accompanying descriptions at parents' night or for another class.

3. Related activities Man Oh Man, Dig Them Bones! on page 114, My Dinosaur Name Is . . . on page 118, and Mystery Footprints on page 122.

MYSTERY FOOTPRINTS _____

PRIMARY CONTENT

- Interpreting events and conditions in the geologic past based on observable evidence
- Developing defensible hypotheses

PRIOR STUDENT KNOWLEDGE

A basic introduction to dinosaurs; suggested completion of the activity Man Oh Man, Dig Them Bones! on page 114

PRE-ACTIVITY PREPARATION

Make an overhead transparency using Fossil Footprint Puzzle 1 Transparency Master (page 125).

PROCESS SKILLS

Observing, comparing, inferring, communicating, hypothesizing, identifying variables

GROUP SIZE

1–4 students

MATERIALS PER GROUP

- 1 overhead projector (for whole class)
- 1 prepared overhead transparency of Fossil Footprint Puzzle 1 (for whole class)

TEACHER INFORMATION

In making interpretations and hypotheses in this activity, students have a tendency to want to ignore the environmental or physical setting. Encourage them to include such aspects whenever possible. For example, the existence of tracks suggests the presence of mud, which implies fine-grained sediment and a wet, humid climate. Exceptions can occur, of course, but the implication is certainly there. A hill might be hypothesized as existing on the left side of the track area. This would explain the widened pace of the larger animal and the reason that the two animals did not see each other initially (if, indeed, they were present at the same time). On the other hand, perhaps the land was flat. The animals could have initially been separated by a stand of trees—one that kept the small animal from seeing the large animal until it was too late (according to one hypothesis), but one that the large animal could look over and see the smaller dinosaur, the widened pace of the larger being a result of the ensuing chase.

An imaginative student should develop several defensible hypotheses. One of the most obvious being that a small animal was caught by a larger animal, they fought, and the smaller one was killed. However, one cannot be certain that they fought to the death, although the disappearance of one set of tracks indicates this to be a strong possibility. Perhaps the smaller animal was a flying reptile that escaped after a brief skirmish by flying away, or perhaps it escaped by running off in a direction in which there was solid rock and no mud to preserve its tracks. Maybe it was a happy event with a large mother dinosaur catching her rambunctious baby and carrying it away.

In fact, there is no evidence to say, for certain, that the tracks were even made at the same time! They could have been made at different times, without the two animals ever having seen each other. Both animals might have seen the same carcass and had themselves solitary meals—at different times. The widened pace of the larger animal might be due to its seeing the carcass from a distance and then running to it. The smaller animal might not have seen the meal until it virtually stumbled on it. The absence of the small animal's tracks after its meal could also be explained in several ways.

There are, therefore, a number of different interpretations of the evidence. Any hypothesis that is logical and consistent with all the evidence is a possibility. While it is true that some interpretations may be stronger than others (the predator/prey hypothesis, for example), no reasonable, logical idea can be totally ruled out unless evidence so dictates.

This is an excellent activity to illustrate the formation, development, and modification of actual scientific interpretations and hypotheses based on the systematic discovery of evidence.

PROCEDURE

1. Introduce the activity by asking students how detectives recreate the scenes of crimes. Lead students to the conclusion that detectives rely on observed clues or evidence. Tell students that today they are going to be dinosaur detectives, searching for clues that will help recreate a prehistoric scene. Explain that their hypotheses will be explanations of what they think happened, based on the evidence. Point out that they, like good detectives, will need to consider all possible explanations of the evidence and not limit themselves to just one favorite hypothesis.

2. Divide the class into groups and project Part One of the Fossil Footprint Puzzle 1 transparency. Use a sheet of paper to cover and block out the other two parts of the transparency. Tell students that these are definitely fossilized dinosaur tracks—but give no further information.

3. Instruct groups that, after careful study and analysis of all the clues, they are to develop one or more hypotheses that reconstructs the scene (both physically and biologically) represented by the tracks in Part One. Tell groups to be as detailed as possible and to be ready to cite reasons (evidence) for each part of their hypothesis or hypotheses. Allow five to ten minutes for this task.

4. Conduct a session during which groups can present their hypotheses, interpretations, and supporting evidence to the class. Give students freedom to question and debate, with you serving as moderator. Accept any explanation as long as it is consistent with the evidence but point out flaws in explanations that are not consistent. Do not directly present any alternative hypotheses or explanations; if necessary, however, you may drop hints by asking leading questions (see step 9).

5. Announce that new evidence has been discovered. Then expose Part Two of the transparency (Part 1 and Part 2 should both be visible now).

6. Advise students that with the discovery of new evidence, they may want to modify their hypothesis or hypotheses, add new ones, or totally discard old ones that are no longer supported by the additional evidence. Again, groups should be as detailed as possible and be ready to list reasons for each hypothesis modification, addition, and/or deletion. Allow five to ten minutes for this task.

7. Repeat step 4.

8. Announce that even more new evidence has been discovered. Expose Part Three of the transparency (the complete puzzle, all three parts, should be visible now). Repeat the instructions given in step 6. Again allow five to ten minutes for this task.

(continues)

(continued)

9. Should it become necessary to stimulate students' thinking at any given stage of the activity, you may ask questions such as the following (there are a number of other questions that you can add to this list):

- What kinds of animals were involved? *(dinosaurs)*

- How many animals were involved? *(two)*

- How did the animals compare in size? *(one large and one small, based on footprint size)*

- Were all the animals adults? *(maybe or maybe not)*

- Were the different sets of tracks made at the same time? *(maybe)* At different times? *(maybe)*

- In what direction did the animals move? Did they change direction? *(The large one initially moved right to left on the overhead, then changed direction and moved left to right. The small one moved left to right.)*

- Did the animals change speed? *(Possibly the large one increased speed, as evidenced by a wider track spacing.)*

- Was the land level or irregular? *(could have been either)*

- What might have caused a change in the track spacing of the larger animal? *(increase in speed or movement up a slope or hill)*

- Was the soil moist or dry when the tracks were made? *(moist)*

- Were the sediments coarse or fine where the tracks were made? *(fine, mud)*

10. Now repeat step 4 once more. This time, however, alert students to any alternative hypotheses or explanations that they may not have suggested. Attempt to make students understand that several different hypotheses could explain the evidence shown in the complete puzzle. Even though some hypotheses may be more likely than others, students (and scientists!) must resist the urge to pick a favorite to the total exclusion of all other possibilities. In essence, there is no right answer to the puzzle—nor will there ever be unless more evidence is discovered.

11. Inform students that this activity reflects the process that accompanies many scientific endeavors in all the disciplines.

EXTENSIONS AND ADAPTATIONS

1. If students have developed good writing skills, you may wish to ask for written reports or explanations in procedure steps 4, 7, and 10.

2. Repeat the activity using Fossil Footprint Puzzle 2 Transparency Master on page 126. You'll be surprised at how refined the students' thinking has become since they have had the experience with Fossil Footprint Puzzle 1.

3. Allow students to draw their own footprint puzzles to try out on each other.

4. Related activities Man Oh Man, Dig Them Bones! on page 114, My Dinosaur Name Is . . . on page 118, and Dinosaur Diorama on page 120.

MYSTERY FOOTPRINTS _____

FOSSIL FOOTPRINT PUZZLE 1
TRANSPARENCY MASTER

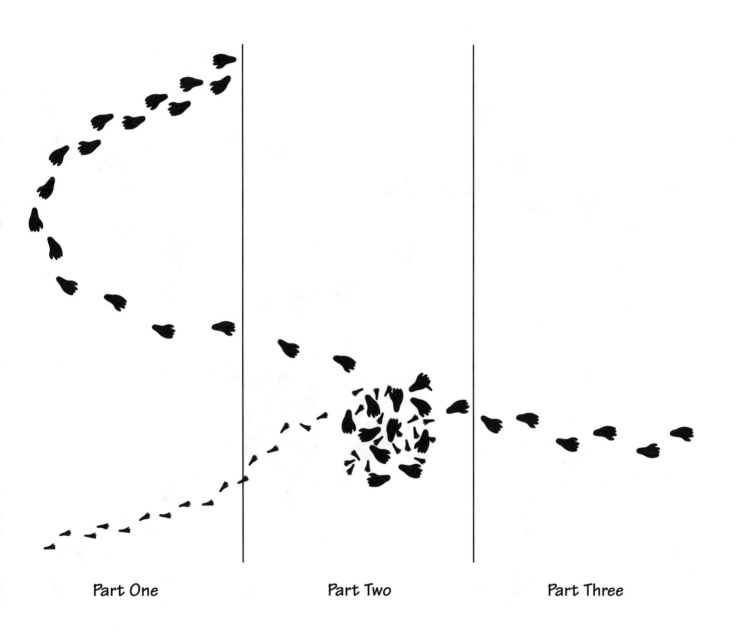

Part One   Part Two   Part Three

MYSTERY FOOTPRINTS

FOSSIL FOOTPRINT PUZZLE 2
TRANSPARENCY MASTER

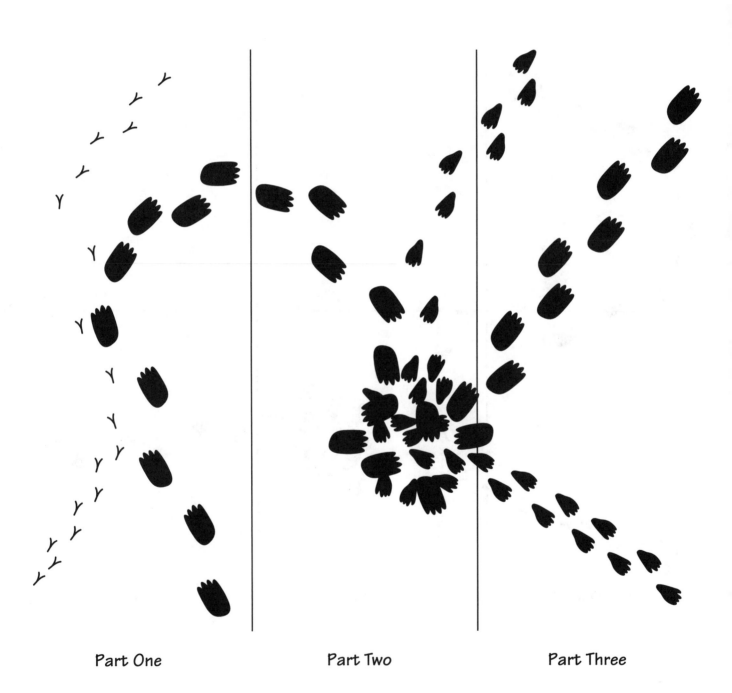

Part One   Part Two   Part Three

A MITE TITE IS ALRITE _____

PRIMARY CONTENT

Formation of stalactites, stalagmites, and columns

PRIOR STUDENT KNOWLEDGE

No special prior knowledge is required.

PRE-ACTIVITY PREPARATION

1. Obtain Epsom salts (available at most drug stores), enough to provide each group with roughly 237 mL (1 c).
2. Obtain a ball of soft, thin cotton yarn, enough to give each group a 76 cm (30 in.) length.
3. Collect enough small rocks to supply each group with 2 rocks. Rinse the rocks if they are dirty. The rocks will be used as weights around which yarn is tied (see illustration in the Procedure).
4. Have students bring from home enough plastic snap-on lids (roughly the size that comes on small margarine tubs) to supply 1 lid to each group.

PROCESS SKILLS

Observing, inferring, hypothesizing, experimenting

GROUP SIZE

2–3 students

MATERIALS PER GROUP

- 2 plastic cups, 473 mL (16 oz)
- Masking tape (for whole class)
- 1 pencil or marker
- Hot tap water or water heated on a hot plate (for whole class)
- 1 plastic cup containing about 237 mL (1 c) of Epsom salts
- 2 plastic spoons
- 2 small rocks
- 1 length of soft, thin cotton yarn, 76 cm (30 in.)
- 1 plastic snap-on lid
- 1 sheet of paper (if writing skills allow)

TEACHER INFORMATION

A cave is a natural passageway in soluble bedrock, most often limestone. Most caves are formed by the solution (dissolving) of limestone by groundwater along zones where groundwater flow is concentrated or intensified—usually fractures, joints, and bedding planes. Limestone is soluble in groundwater because of dissolved atmospheric carbon dioxide that entered the water when it fell as rain. The presence of CO_2 in water causes it to become a weak carbonic acid. It is this acid that reacts with the limestone causing it to dissolve.

Once a cave is created and becomes air-filled as a result of the lowering of the water table, water from above seeps and drips into the cave. As a water drop hangs on the ceiling, some of it evaporates, leaving a deposit of calcium carbonate that the water had dissolved from the limestone during its journey down to the cave. With continued dripping from the same spot, an icicle-shaped formation is created called a stalactite (mnemonic: it hangs "tite" to the ceiling). When drops fall and hit the cave floor, additional evaporation and deposition occur. This results in a

(continues)

(continued)

more blunted icicle-shaped formation rising up from the floor—a stalagmite (mnemonic: it "mite" grow up someday). When a stalactite and a stalagmite grow to meet and combine, they form a column.

In this activity, the salt solution travels along the yarn by capillary action and drips from the low point of the yarn sag onto the lid. If this happens at the right rate, and if the surrounding conditions are appropriate, evaporation at the sag and lid results in the precipitation and accumulation of Epsom salts crystals. This finally results in forms that resemble stalactites and stalagmites—and eventually columns. Both the success of, and the time required for, formation growth range considerably, depending on solution, yarn, and room conditions. However, the major caution in this activity is not to get too big (deep) a sag in the yarn, which would cause the dripping to occur too fast, not allowing enough time for evaporation and crystal growth.

PROCEDURE

1. Prime students by asking questions such as:

   - Have any of you ever been in a real cave?

   - Did you see cave formations?

   - Were they all the same or were there different kinds?

   - Can you describe what they looked like?

   - Do you remember the names of some of the cave formations?

   - How do you think caves form?

   - How do you think cave formations form?

2. Use the last two questions to generate a discussion about cave development, including the description of and the origin of the three most common cave formations: stalactites, stalagmites, and columns (see Teacher Information).

3. Tell students that today they will begin an activity in which they will try to actually grow stalactites, stalagmites, and columns.

4. Group students and distribute the materials. Each group should place on one of its empty cups a strip of masking tape displaying the group members' initials.

5. Have each group fill both cups about three-fourths with hot water. Water of a temperature normally used for washing hands is both safe and adequate.

6. Have each group add Epsom salts to both cups of water simultaneously, a spoonful at a time. After each spoonful, students should stir the water until the salt is dissolved. Groups are to continue this process until no more salt will dissolve in the water. It is very important that the water in both cups be fully saturated with Epsom salts. Consequently, tell students not to give up on the dissolving process too soon—only after the salt will no longer dissolve after at least three minutes of constant stirring. Make additional salt available to any group that runs out.

7. Instruct each group to tie one rock to each end of the length of yarn. Assist groups as necessary.

8. Students should now move the cups of solution, the weighted yarn, and the plastic lid to a location in the classroom where they can remain undisturbed for five to fourteen days. Students will complete the setup at that location.

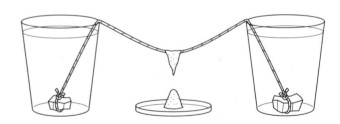

9. Tell each group to place its cups about 8 cm–10 cm (3 in.–4 in.) apart, with the plastic lid positioned directly between the cups. Students are then to place one weighted end of yarn in each cup. The section of yarn that extends between the 2 cups should be in the form of a gentle droop or sag, the low point of the sag being positioned directly above the plastic lid.

10. If the yarn will not stay in a gentle sag because of too much slack, have students take up some slack by either spreading the cups farther apart or by removing one end of the yarn and shortening it.

11. Inform students that the setups will remain undisturbed for five to fourteen days. Then have each student develop a prediction as to what will happen and why. Students can share their predictions verbally, or you may ask that they each record them on a sheet of paper.

12. During the wait time, allow students to observe on a daily basis the progress of formation growth. A stalactite should begin developing first, followed by a stalagmite. With a little luck and patience, the two formations will grow together into a column.

13. At the conclusion of the activity, review with students the process by which the setups produced cave formations (see Teacher Information).

EXTENSIONS AND ADAPTATIONS

1. This activity is appropriate for use in a learning center.

2. If you wish, you can do this activity as a whole-class experience using a single setup.

3. Invite other classes to view the cave formations at various stages of growth.

4. Try the activity using powdered alum in place of Epsom salts.

5. Obtain slides, videos, or movies of caves and cave formations to show to the class.

6. If a commercial cave is accessible, arrange a field trip.

7. Related activity Sinking on page 130.

SINKING

PRIMARY CONTENT

- Understanding sinkhole formation
- Understanding the development of karst topography

PRIOR STUDENT KNOWLEDGE

Exposure to the concept of the solubility of limestone by ground water and the concept of the formation of caves; suggested completion of the activity A Mite Tite Is Alrite on page 127

PRE-ACTIVITY PREPARATION

1. Ask students to bring from home: clean pump-spray plastic bottles (any size); 1.89 L ($\frac{1}{2}$ gal) cardboard milk cartons; and coffee cans, about 10 cm (4 in.) in diameter. Students should bring in enough to supply each group with 1 of each of the 3 kinds of containers. Cut the tops off the milk cartons to make them about 10 cm (4 in.) high. Then use a compass point or nail to poke into the bottom of the cartons about 10 drainage holes within a 3 in. diameter circle.

2. Each group will need about 590 mL ($2\frac{1}{2}$ c) of fine sand. You can collect sand or obtain it at a garden supply center.

3. Collect several pictures or slides showing sinkholes. Check sources such as geology texts, earth science texts, and encyclopedias.

PROCESS SKILLS

Observing, inferring, hypothesizing, experimenting

GROUP SIZE

2–3 students

MATERIALS PER GROUP

- 1 pump-spray plastic bottle
- Available water (for whole class)
- 12 sugar cubes
- 1 prepared milk carton (see Pre-Activity Preparation)
- 1 coffee can
- Approximately 590 mL ($2\frac{1}{2}$ c) of fine sand
- Pictures of sinkholes (for whole class)
- 1 sink or disposal bucket (for whole class)

TEACHER INFORMATION

Sinkholes are surface depressions that resemble craters or pits, and they pockmark landscapes where caves are present beneath the surface. Areas having numerous sinkholes and caves are known as karst regions (or karst topography). Sinkholes can range in size from a few feet in diameter and depth to in excess of 500 feet in diameter and over 125 feet in depth! Sinkholes develop in two ways. Some develop gradually over many years without any physical disturbance to the rock. These form when limestone immediately below the soil is slowly dissolved by downward seeping rainwater. Called solution sinks, these depressions are usually shallow and have gently sloping sides. Collapse sinks, on the other hand, form suddenly when the roof of a cavern collapses under the weight of overlying material. Collapse sinks are typically steep-sided and deep. Although responses to the last two questions in step 9 of the Procedure focus on collapse sinks, the sinkholes formed in this activity may be of either type, depending on how the solution of the sugar progresses. You should, therefore, adjust desired responses accordingly.

PROCEDURE

1. If necessary, review with students the fact that limestone, a common rock comprising bedrock, is soluble in groundwater—the result often being the formation of caves.

2. Show students pictures of sinkholes and discuss the definition of *sinkhole* and the descriptive characteristics of sinkholes and karst topography (see Teacher Information). Ask students if they can guess how sinkholes might be formed.

3. After students have shared their ideas, indicate that in today's activity they will investigate sinkhole formation.

4. Group students and distribute the materials. Have each group fill its spray bottle with water. Then provide instructions as delineated in steps 5–8.

5. Have each group center 4 sugar cubes in a single 2 x 2 cube layer in the bottom of the milk carton. Have students use their remaining cubes to make the stack 3 layers high.

6. Ask each group to slowly fill the carton with sand (trying not to disturb the sugar cubes) until the sand reaches a level about 1.3 cm ($\frac{1}{2}$ in.) above the sugar cubes.

7. Each group should then carefully set the carton on the coffee can so that the corners of the carton rest on the rim of the can.

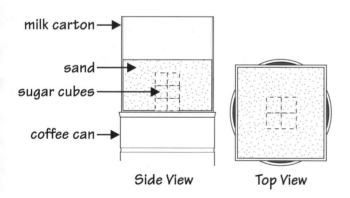

Side View   Top View

8. Tell each group to set the pump on the bottle to spray (as opposed to stream), if possible. Group members should then take turns spraying water over the surface of the sand. They should spray for thirty seconds and then stop for a few seconds and observe the sand. Have them keep repeating this procedure to see if a sinkhole develops. If one does form, they should continue applying water until the sinkhole stops increasing in size. (It typically takes between five and fifteen minutes for sinkhole formation to occur, depending on the rate of water application.)

9. After groups have observed sinkhole formation, review results through questions such as:

   • What do the stacked sugar cubes represent in your model? *(limestone bedrock)*

   • How are the sugar cubes like limestone bedrock? *(Both are soluble; both are layered; and both have vertical joints.)*

   • What does the sand represent? *(loose, unconsolidated material [soil] overlying bedrock)*

   • What did the spraying of water represent? *(rain)*

   • Where did the sinkhole first start appearing? *(directly over the stacked sugar cubes)*

   • What caused the sinkhole to form? *(As water filtered downward, it dissolved the sugar—especially along joints and layer boundaries where concentrated flow occurred—and created a cavity or cave in the cubes. As the cave increased in size, a point was reached where its roof could no longer support the weight of the overlying material. The roof thus collapsed, causing the surface material to drop into the cave. This formed a depression in the surface which is the sinkhole.)*

   • Can you see how real sinkholes would form in the natural environment? *(Yes, like sugar, limestone would dissolve and create caves. If the caves grew too large, overlying rock and soil would collapse into the caves and form sinkholes.)*

EXTENSIONS AND ADAPTATIONS

1. This activity is appropriate for use in a learning center.

2. Assist students with looking up information about one of the most publicized and famous sinkhole occurrences: the sudden collapse of the surface in an urban area that created the huge Winter Park, Florida, sinkhole—on May 8, 1981.

3. If you are located in a karst area, take students on a field trip to observe actual sinkholes.

4. Related activity A Mite Tite Is Alrite on page 127.

Earth Science Activities (KSAM)

ASTRONOMY

- MOON
- STARS AND CONSTELLATIONS

MOON MAN

PRIMARY CONTENT

The phases of the moon

PRIOR STUDENT KNOWLEDGE

Knowledge that the moon is only a reflector, not a producer, of light and that the moon is visible only as a consequence of sunlight reflected off its surface

PRE-ACTIVITY PREPARATION

1. Obtain a baseball-size or softball-size white plastic ball (available at most craft or hobby supply stores) or a similar-size white solid rubber ball. Divide the ball into two halves by encircling the ball with a strip of masking tape, with one edge of the tape marking the line between the two halves. Continue applying tape to that half until the half is completely covered. Spray paint the uncovered half with a flat (not glossy) black paint. When the paint has dried, remove the tape. You will now have a half-black and half-white moon model. Make a holder for the model by forcing a sharp pencil or skewer into the ball at any point on the black/white boundary.

2. Copy reproducible Moon-Phase Tester (page 139), one copy per student.

PROCESS SKILLS

Observing, classifying, inferring

GROUP SIZE

Whole class, followed by individual

MATERIALS PER GROUP

- Scissors
- 1 copy of reproducible Moon-Phase Tester for each student
- Glue
- 1 sheet of black construction paper
- Crayons
- 13 small stick-on stars (or suitable substitute) in 5 colors: 2 of color A, 2 of color B, 3 of color C, 3 of color D, and 3 of color E (see steps 4 and 5 in the Part Two Procedure)
- 1 single-edge razor blade or craft knife (for teacher use)
- 1 thick section of cardboard (for teacher use)
- 1 moon model (for teacher demonstration) (see Pre-Activity Preparation)

TEACHER INFORMATION

It takes $29\frac{1}{2}$ solar days for the moon to make a complete revolution around the earth. Although half of the moon (the half facing the sun) is always illuminated by the sun due to reflected light, the lighted portion appears to change shape (as viewed from earth) during revolution. This is due to changes in the relative positions of the earth, sun, and moon during lunar revolution. During the first half of the moon's orbit, its apparent shape grows (waxes) through the following phases: new-moon phase (not visible); waxing-crescent phase (right side visible as a crescent moon); first-quarter phase (right side visible

(continues)

(continued)

as a half moon); waxing-gibbous phase (right side visible as a three-fourths moon); and full-moon phase (visible as a full round circle). During the remaining half of the lunar orbit, it decreases (wanes) in size. After a full moon, it progresses through the following phases: waning-gibbous phase (left side visible as a three-fourths moon); third-quarter phase (left side visible as a half moon); waning-crescent phase (left side visible as a crescent moon); and then back again to the new-moon phase to start another cycle.

Two simplifications in lunar-phase terminology are suggested for students at the 2–3 level, and both are incorporated into the activity. (a) Since waxing phases (shapes) look identical to waning phases (except for the side of the moon that is illuminated), corresponding waxing and waning phases are presented as a single phase. For example, the waxing-crescent phase and the waning-crescent phase are not differentiated; instead, both are simply referred to as the crescent phase. (b) The first- and third-quarter phases actually appear as half moons. This can be very confusing to young students. Consequently both are referred to simply as half-moon phase instead of first-quarter phase and third-quarter phase. Unless your objectives dictate otherwise, it is usually better for overall concept attainment if the preceding terminology differentiation is reserved for a higher grade level.

PROCEDURE

Part One: A Demonstration of Lunar Phases

1. If necessary, review with students the concept of producers and reflectors of light. Also review the fact that the sun, like other stars, is a light producer; other celestial bodies, including earth's moon, are primarily reflectors of light.

2. Discuss how the moon orbits the earth at the same time that the earth orbits the sun. Draw a diagram depicting such on the chalkboard (see illustration).

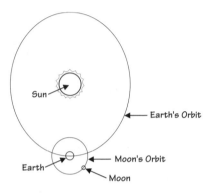

3. Generate discussion about the moon with questions such as:

    - Does the moon always appear to be the same shape?

    - How would you describe the different shapes of the moon that you have seen?

    - Do the actual shape and size of the moon change?

    - Is there really a man in the moon?

    - Is the moon really made of green cheese?

    - What do you think the moon is composed of? (Inform the class that the moon is similar to the earth in that it is composed of solid rock with a thin soil covering—although lunar soil is more powdery [smaller grain size] and lacks vegetative matter.)

    - Do you have any ideas as to why the moon appears to change in shape?

4. Use the last question to introduce the concept of lunar phases through the following demonstration (steps 5–12).

5. Draw and label a large sun on the chalkboard. Have students move their desks away from the center of the room; group the students in the cleared center area. Tell students that they represent the earth, specifically people on the earth looking up into the sky. The sun is in the direction of the chalkboard.

6. Show students the moon model and point out that one half is black and the other half is white. Indicate that the white side represents the side (half) of the moon facing the sun—the side that is reflecting sunlight and can therefore be seen. The black side represents the side (half) of the moon opposite the sun—the side that is in dark shadow and cannot be seen since it is not reflecting sunlight.

7. Holding the moon model up, stand directly between the students (earth) and the chalkboard (sun), shown as position 1 in the diagram. Ask students which way the white (lighted) side of the moon should be facing. *(The lighted side should be facing the sun [chalkboard].)* Position the moon model accordingly and then ask how much of the lighted side of the moon they can see. *(none)* What would the real moon look like from earth? *(It would not be visible.)* Tell students that this is called the new-moon phase.

8. "Orbit" the earth (students) by moving around the perimeter of the room to position 2 and repeat the step 7 questions. *(The lighted side should still directly face the board. Now, students will see a sliver of the lighted side—a distinct crescent moon. The moon's appearance from the student's reference point is shown on the diagram, adjacent to position 2, outside the moon's orbit. These appearance drawings are included for all 8 positions.)* Tell students this is called the crescent phase.

9. Orbit to position 3 and repeat the questions. *(The lighted side should still face the board. Now, students will see half of the lighted side—a distinct half moon.)* Tell students this is called the half-moon phase.

10. Orbit to position 4 and repeat the questions. *(The lighted side still faces the board. Now, students will see most, but not all, of the lighted side—kind of a three-fourths moon.)* Tell students this is called the gibbous phase.

11. Orbit to position 5 and repeat the questions. *(The lighted side still faces the board. Now, students will see all of the lighted side—a distinct full moon.)* Tell students this is called the full-moon phase.

12. Complete the demonstration by orbiting to positions 6, 7, and 8 and repeating the questions at each position. *(The lighted side should still directly face the board in all positions. Students will again see a gibbous phase in position 6, another half-moon phase in position 7, and another crescent phase in position 8.)*

(continues)

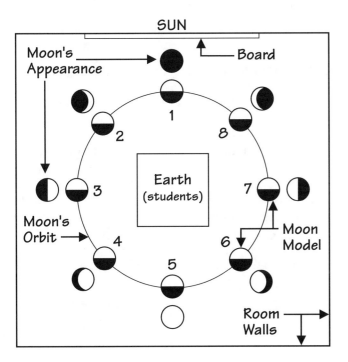

(continued)

Part Two: Making a Moon-Phase Tester

1. While distributing materials to each student, indicate that students are now each going to make a moon-phase tester that will help them learn the different lunar phases.

2. Have students each cut out the moon (circle) from the reproducible and glue it onto the sheet of black construction paper. Have students each use a light-colored crayon to write their initials on the back of the construction paper.

3. After the glue has dried, collect all the portions containing the moon.

4. Tell students each to detach the two strips from the bottom portion of the reproducible by cutting along the dashed lines. After students have separated the strips, they should assign a star-sticker color to each of the five lunar phases, for example: new—blue; crescent—silver; half—gold; gibbous—red; full—yellow.

5. Students are to attach the appropriate-colored star directly behind (on the backside of the strip) each of the five moon-phase names on that strip. They should then do the same thing behind the drawings on the moon-phase appearance strip. For example, using the colors given in step 4, they would place a silver star behind the term *crescent-moon phase;* likewise, they would place a silver star behind each of the two drawings (appearances) of a crescent moon on the other strip. They should repeat the process with blue stars for a new moon (only one drawing of that phase) and so on for all the phases.

6. While students are busy working on steps 4 and 5, use a single-edge razor blade or a craft knife to cut four slits (along the four dashed lines) in each student's moon. Then completely cut out the two little windows (dotted lines) located between the slits in each student's moon. Do the cutting on a thick section of cardboard. With a sharp blade, this cutting task proceeds very rapidly.

7. Return the moons to the students. Allow students to draw on and color their moons however they wish (lunar craters, a human face in the moon, and so on). Also let them use white and/or yellow crayons to draw features in the blackness of space around the moon (stars, comets, and so on).

8. Have each student insert each strip through the slits on the moon—from the backside through the top slit and over the windows, then from the front side through the bottom slit—so that one phase appearance and one phase name appear side-by-side (see illustration, shown without the construction paper).

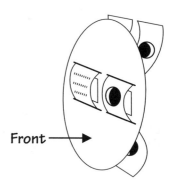

Front →

9. With their moon-phase testers, students can test themselves or other students by matching different moon appearances with corresponding phase names. They can check each match by seeing if the star colors on the back of the tester match.

EXTENSIONS AND ADAPTATIONS

1. If desired, you can do Parts One and Two as separate activities on different days.

2. Collect pictures of the actual moon in different phases and have students identify the phases.

3. Have students observe the moon for a specified number of nights and then report on the phases that they observed.

4. See Extensions activity 5 in the activity Star Gazer on page 147 with regard to using the stargazer telescope for viewing lunar phases.

MOON MAN

MOON-PHASE TESTER

Name

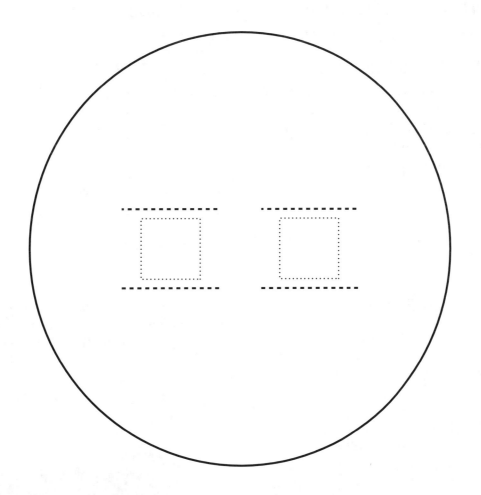

Half-
Moon
Phase

Full-
Moon
Phase

Gibbous-
Moon
Phase

New-
Moon
Phase

Crescent-
Moon
Phase

STAR PICTURES _____

PRIMARY CONTENT
Introducing constellations

PRIOR STUDENT KNOWLEDGE
No special prior knowledge is required.

PRE-ACTIVITY PREPARATION
1. Copy reproducible Mystery Constellation (page 142), two copies per student
2. Copy reproducibles Cepheus (page 143), Big Dipper (page 144), and Draco (page 145), one copy of each per student.

PROCESS SKILLS
Observing, classifying

GROUP SIZE
Individual

MATERIALS PER GROUP
- 2 copies of reproducible Mystery Constellation
- 1 pencil or marker
- Crayons
- 1 copy of reproducible Cepheus
- 1 copy of reproducible Big Dipper
- 1 copy of reproducible Draco

TEACHER INFORMATION

The night sky has changed very little throughout human history. Although both the earth and the stars are in motion, the stars appear fixed and unchanging to us because they are so distant from the earth. Early astronomers looked at stars and grouped them into patterns called constellations. Due to the tremendous number of stars, not all stars are included in constellations. Do not be surprised if some constellations appear different on different star charts. This is due to interpretation. The names of constellations were based on familiar animals, objects, or mythical figures. Though it must have taken a great deal of imagination for the originators to see the various figures, shapes, and characters among the stars, many (if not most) constellations do not look a great deal like what they are suppose to represent. As a consequence, a number of the more famous constellations have taken on secondary or informal

names that seem to more accurately describe the star patterns. For example, this activity includes the group of stars known as the Big Dipper. The Big Dipper is actually part of Ursa Major which means "the Great Bear." The other two constellations included in this activity are Cepheus (the king) and Draco (the dragon).

PROCEDURE

1. Introduce the activity by asking students questions such as:

   - Have you ever observed clouds and tried to pick out different shapes or figures created by the cloud formations?

   - Do the cloud figures look exactly like what you think they represent? *(No, clouds only form likenesses, not exact replicas; most of the time you use your imagination a little to "see" the cloud figures.)*

   - Have you ever stared at the stars and done the same thing (picked out shapes or figures)?

2. Distribute one copy of Mystery Constellation to each student. Instruct students to join the stars with lines, as in a dot-to-dot picture, to create any shape or figure that they might see. They may or may not use all the stars shown. Tell students that, as with cloud pictures, they may have to use their imaginations to "see" shapes or figures. One very simple shape, a box, is shown at the top of the sheet. (There are no right or wrong solutions; the possibilities are endless, depending upon the number of stars used and students' imagination.)

3. When students have finished, have them each name (or describe) their figure on the lines provided. Then ask them to color their figure and the remainder of the star sheet in any way they wish.

4. Explain to the class that throughout history, people have looked at the stars and used their imaginations to form pictures—much as the students have just done. Ask if anyone knows what name is given to a grouping of stars that creates a picture. *(constellation)*

5. Tell the class that you would like them to try and locate some real constellations. Then distribute to each student one copy of each of the reproducibles Cepheus, Big Dipper, and Draco.

6. On each star sheet, the constellation is shown in a small box at the top of the page. Students should try to locate that constellation among the stars in the larger box. For example, after examining the boxed picture of Cepheus, students should try to find that constellation on the page. Then they should depict the constellation by drawing lines to connect the stars that make up the constellation. Students should note that not all the stars shown in the box are a part of Cepheus. Students should then follow the same procedure for the other two constellations. Note that Draco has been made a little more challenging than the others.

7. When students have finished, review the correct solutions (see Answer Keys on page 155).

8. Now give each student a second copy of Mystery Constellation and have them again design and name a constellation. Students should not use the same figures that they used on the first copy.

9. Conduct a discussion of constellations through questions such as the following (see Teacher Information):

   - Who can review what a constellation is?

   - How do you think constellations got their names?

   - How did people decide on what stars to group together to make a constellation?

   - Are all the stars in the sky grouped into constellations?

   - Do you think constellations always look exactly like what they represent?

EXTENSIONS AND ADAPTATIONS

1. This activity is appropriate for use in a learning center.

2. Make additional star pictures that students can use in an attempt to identify constellations. You can select constellations from the reproducible Chart of Selected Constellations in the activity Stargazer on page 147. You can then add additional stars around each selected constellation to hide it. You can make the star pictures simple or challenging by limiting or by increasing the number of surrounding stars.

3. Have students look up information in appropriate sources regarding constellations. Students might find the meaning of constellation names to be especially interesting.

4. Related activity Stargazer on page 147.

STAR PICTURES _____

MYSTERY CONSTELLATION

Name_____

Figure name or description: _____

_____

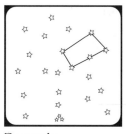

Example

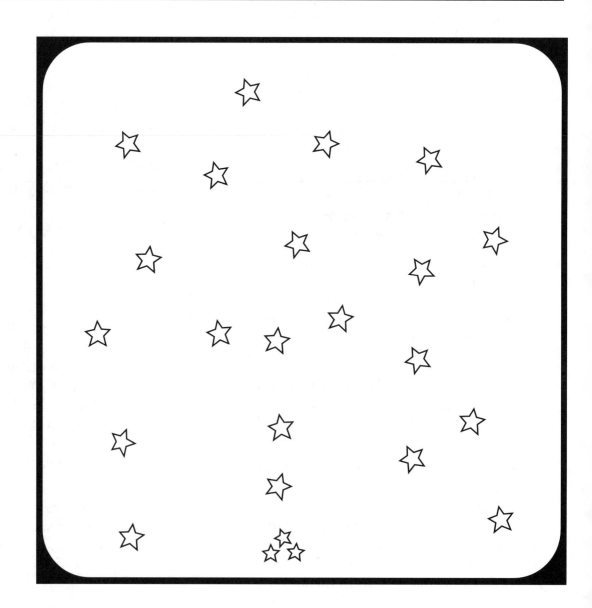

STAR PICTURES

CEPHEUS

Name

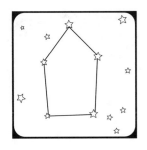

STAR PICTURES

BIG DIPPER

Name_____

©Curriculum Associates, Inc.   *Earth Science Activities (KSAM)*

STAR PICTURES _____

DRACO

Name _____

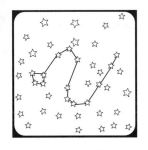

STARGAZER

PRIMARY CONTENT

- Recognizing the sun and stars
- Identifying selected constellations
- Constructing a stargazer telescope

PRIOR STUDENT KNOWLEDGE

Basic introduction to constellations; suggested completion of the activity Star Pictures on page 140

PRE-ACTIVITY PREPARATION

1. Collect enough 224 g (8 oz) potato chip cans with clear plastic lids to supply 1 to each student. Ask students to bring these from home. Once collected, use a hammer and a large (#12 or #16) nail to punch a hole in the center of the metal end of each can. Widen the holes a little more by reaming with the nail.
2. Obtain enough #3 and #6 finishing nails to supply each student with one of each.
3. From old boxes, cut for each student a section of corrugated cardboard measuring at least 23 cm x 30.5 cm (9 in. x 12 in.).
4. Copy reproducibles Telescope Constellations 1 (page 150), Telescope Constellations 2 (page 151), and Chart of Selected Constellations (page 152), one copy of each per student.

PROCESS SKILLS

Observing, classifying

GROUP SIZE

Individual

MATERIALS PER GROUP

- 1 copy of reproducible Telescope Constellations 1
- 1 copy of reproducible Telescope Constellations 2
- 2 sheets of black construction paper, 23 cm x 30.5 cm (9 in. x 12 in.)
- 1 stapler (for teacher use)
- 1 sharpened pencil
- 1 section of corrugated cardboard, at least 23 x 30.5 cm (9 in. x 12 in.)
- 1 white crayon
- One #6 finishing nail
- One #3 finishing nail
- 1 potato chip-type can, 224 g (8 oz), with lid
- Scissors
- 1 copy of reproducible Chart of Selected Constellations

TEACHER INFORMATION

The night sky has changed very little throughout human history. Although both the earth and the stars are in motion, the stars appear fixed and unchanging to us because they are so distant from the earth. Early astronomers looked at stars and grouped them into patterns called constellations. The names of constellations were based on familiar animals, objects, or mythical figures. Due to the tremendous number of stars, not all stars are included in constellations.

(continues)

(continued)

Stars are the primary constituents of the universe. Stars are grouped into galaxies. Just within sight of our telescopes, there are hundreds of billions of galaxies, each one containing hundreds of billions of stars! Stars are gaseous bodies composed of mostly hydrogen and a little helium. Stars produce their own light through the conversion of hydrogen into helium, a thermonuclear fusion process that results in a tremendous output of energy. The sun is a rather average star in virtually all aspects. It appears to us to be so much larger and brighter than other stars only because of its nearness to earth—an average distance of only 150 million km (93 million mi). Other stars are located tens, hundreds, thousands, and millions of light years from earth! One light year equals about 9.5 trillion km (5.8 trillion mi). Although only an average-sized star, the sun is gigantic compared to the earth. Students may find it amazing to know that the sun would hold over $1\frac{1}{4}$ million earths inside of it! Contrary to what most people think, the stars are present in the daytime sky just as they are in the nighttime sky. During the day, however, the brightness of the sun is overpowering and prevents stars from being seen.

PROCEDURE

1. Open the activity with a discussion of stars. Include questions such as those that follow, introducing explanations and additional information as necessary (see Teacher Information).

   - What is a star? What are stars made of?

   - Are stars producers or reflectors of light?

   - Is the sun a star? If so, why is it so much larger and brighter than all the other stars?

   - Where are the stars during the day? Are they only up in the sky at night?

   - Do you know what a constellation is?

   - How did constellations get their names?

   - Are all stars grouped in constellations?

2. Tell students that stargazing is a very enjoyable and common hobby or pastime. Before stargazing can really be fun, however, you have to have some idea of what you are looking for—a basic knowledge of the shapes or patterns of constellations. Explain that the purpose of today's activity is to learn ten of the most common constellations in a rather unusual way—through the use of stargazer telescopes.

3. Distribute to each student all the materials except the reproducible Chart of Selected Constellations.

4. Have each student place each of his/her 2 telescope constellation charts on top of a black sheet of construction paper. Circulate through the room and staple the corners of each chart to its black backing. Then provide students with the following instructions (steps 5–14).

5. Ask each student to place the chart on a smooth, hard surface and then use a pencil to trace over the circles on each chart. Students should press firmly enough on the pencil to make an indentation in the construction paper below.

6. Tell each student to place one of his/her charts (with the backing) on top of the cardboard section and poke holes cleanly through the star dots in the circles on the chart. Students should use the larger (#6) nail for the larger star dots (brighter stars) and the smaller (#3) nail for the smaller ones (dimmer stars). Have them repeat this procedure for the second chart. (Step 14 suggests an optional approach you may wish students to use for making the holes.)

7. Ask each student to separate the chart from the black paper and then, with a white crayon, copy the constellation outlines (the lines connecting the stars) and the constellation names from the circles on the chart to the corresponding indented circles on the black paper. The outlines and names should be on the smooth side of the black paper, not on the side with the puckers created by punching the holes.

8. Have students repeat steps 6 and 7 for their second charts.

9. Each student should now carefully cut out the circles from both pieces of black paper, trying to make the cuts along the outside edge of the indented lines. If necessary, students should use the nails to reopen any holes within the cutout circles that might have closed during the labeling process.

10. Have each student select any black circle (any constellation) and center the circle over the inside of the plastic lid so that the crayon outline and the constellation name are pointed down into the lid. The circle will be just a little larger than the lid. Students should press the circle into the lid near its center and then work out toward the rim, trying not to press on any of the punched-out holes since that might cause them to close up. The result will be that the edges of the circle will fold upward a little against the edges of the lid, creating a good, lightproof fit (see illustration).

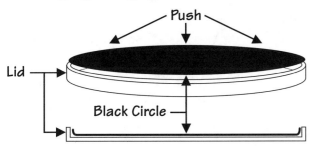

11. Tell students that once they snap the lids onto the cans, they will each have their own stargazer telescope! They should each point the lid of the telescope toward a window or another light source and look through the small hole punched in the other end. They will see a night sky punctuated by the lighted stars of their selected constellation. Point out that they will find this much more fun and realistic than studying constellation drawings on paper! They can check the name of their constellation by looking at the lid-end of the can.

12. Then have each student carefully remove the first circle from the lid and replace it with another constellation. Students can continue until they have learned to recognize and identify all eight constellations. If they wish, they may each pair up with another student so that they can test each other's skill at constellation identification through the stargazer telescopes.

13. Distribute a Chart of Selected Constellations to each student. Read aloud the text on this sheet if necessary. This chart displays additional constellations that students may wish to learn. They may also use it as a reference in constructing more constellation circles for use with their stargazer telescopes.

14. (Optional) The method for punching the holes delineated in step 6 is very simple and works fairly well. The only problem is that the paper puckers created by the punching have a tendency to partially close after repeated use, necessitating their reopening. An alternate method that results in clean holes (no paper puckers) is to substitute a scrap piece of wood for the corrugated cardboard and provide students with hammers. A hole is punched by inverting the nail and placing its head against the paper. With the nail vertical, its point is given one or two good raps with the hammer so that the nail head is driven through the paper and slightly into the wood. Puckerless holes are the result!

EXTENSIONS AND ADAPTATIONS

1. This activity is appropriate for use in a learning center.

2. Encourage students to look at the night sky on their own and try to locate constellations they have learned about in this activity.

3. Conduct a star watch some evening for the whole class.

4. Have students collect plastic lids from the kind of potato chip cans used in the activity. With multiple lids, a constellation can be permanently placed in a lid, eliminating the need for circle replacement each time the student wants to view a different constellation.

5. Black construction paper circles can also be made showing phases of the moon. However, these are more difficult to make and require the use of a single-edge razor blade or craft knife. Consequently, their construction should be attempted only by an adult.

6. Have students look up information in appropriate sources regarding constellations. Students might find the meaning of constellation names to be especially interesting.

7. Related activity Star Pictures on page 140.

STARGAZER

TELESCOPE CONSTELLATIONS 1

Name_____

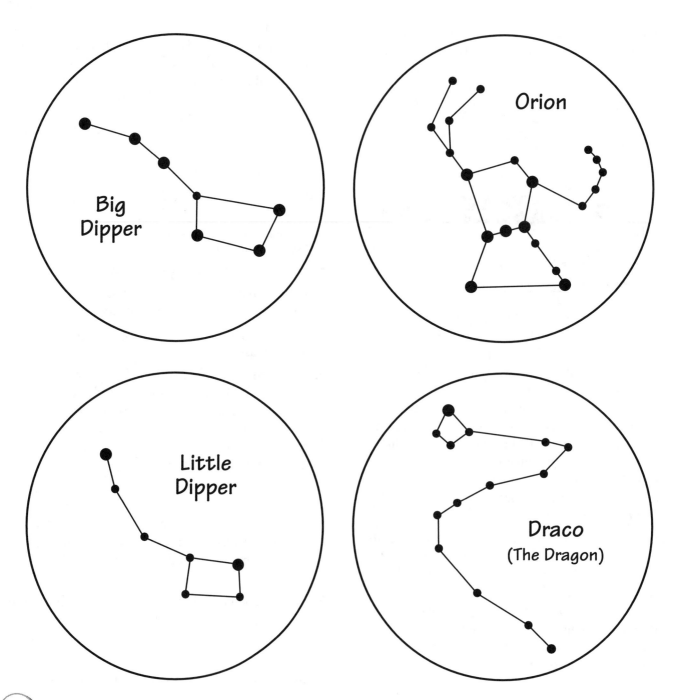

©Curriculum Associates, Inc.   *Earth Science Activities (KSAM)*

STARGAZER

TELESCOPE CONSTELLATIONS 2

Name

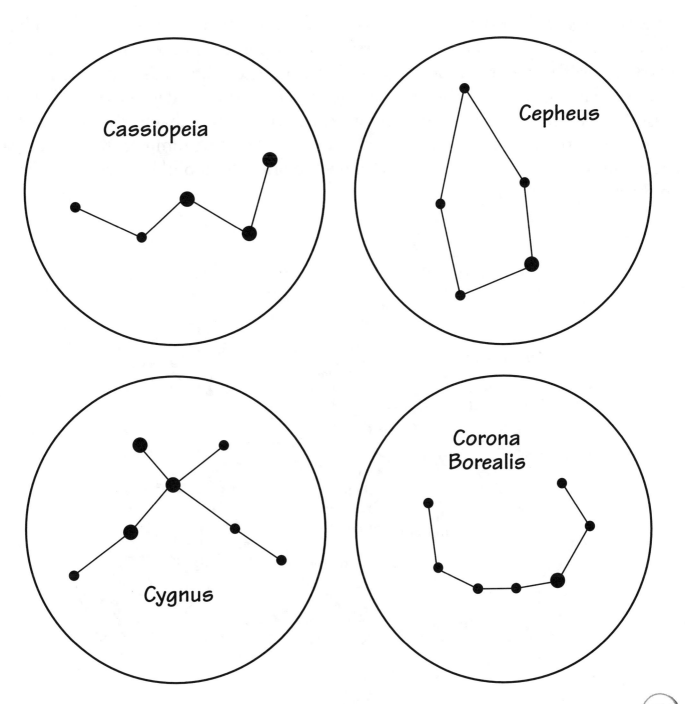

Cassiopeia

Cepheus

Cygnus

Corona
Borealis

STARGAZER

CHART OF SELECTED CONSTELLATIONS

Name_____

This simple star chart shows some Northern Hemisphere constellations. A number of these constellations are only visible during certain seasons. Those at the center of the chart are visible all year at most locations in the United States. Also, the orientation of the constellations to the viewer will change with both time of day and date of viewing. Lastly, star brightness is given in only two categories on this chart—the larger dots representing brighter stars and the smaller dots representing dimmer stars. If you can locate one constellation, the chart will show the orientation of the other constellations to the one you located.

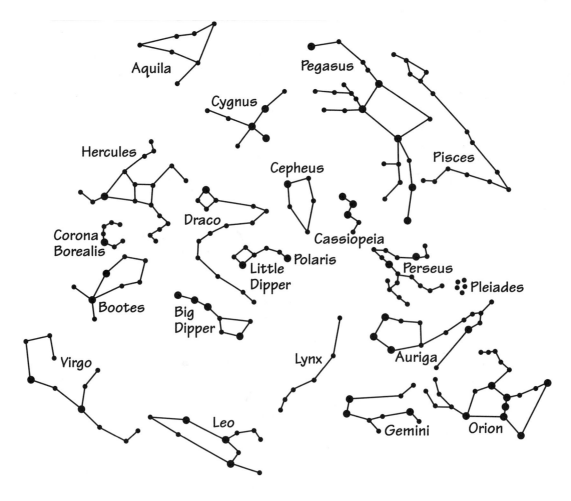

ANSWER KEY

Activity 17: Ahoy Matey
Currents and More Currents (page 61)

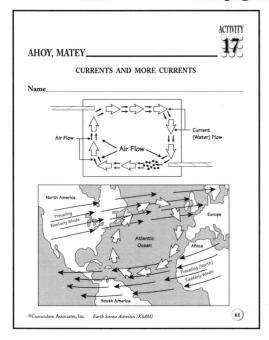

Activity 30: Settle Down!
Sediment Drawing (page 105)

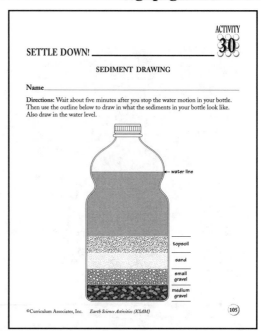

Activity 21: A Squirty Contest
Student Data Sheet (page 75)

Activity 34: Man Oh Man, Dig Them Bones!
Scattered Skeleton Scene (page 117)

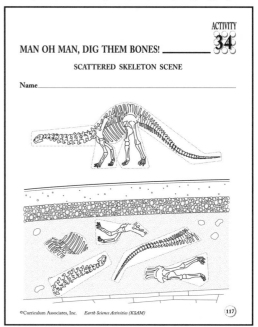

Activity 41: Star Pictures
Cepheus (page 143)

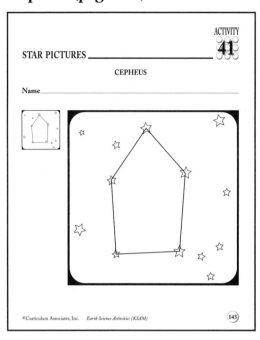

Activity 41: Star Pictures
Draco (page 145)

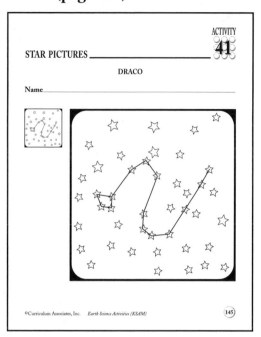

Activity 41: Star Pictures
Big Dipper (page 144)

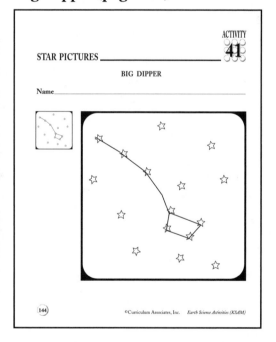

APPENDIX A

APPENDIX A

THE SCIENCE PROCESSES

The number and specific definitions of the science processes vary in the literature depending on the purpose and the degree to which the processes are generalized or detailed. The scientific process skills and definitions listed below are those utilized in this activity guide.

Observing	Using all the senses for the direct and indirect examination of materials or phenomena.
Comparing	Comparing two or more sets of observations, either simultaneously or temporally.
Classifying	Grouping of materials or phenomena based on observed similarities and differences.
Inferring	Making evaluations, drawing conclusions, or making deductions based on observation.
Measuring	Obtaining and expressing quantitative parameters.
Predicting	Suggesting an expected result based upon observations and inferences.
Recording Data	Keeping accurate records in written, numeric, and/or graphic form.
Communicating	Conveying or making available information by describing, drawing, graphing, diagraming, etc.
Hypothesizing	Making or devising a testable prediction.
Identifying Variables	Recognizing factors that could influence the outcome of an event.
Experimenting	Using data-gathering procedures to discover cause and effect relationships.

APPENDIX B

APPENDIX B

THE SCIENCE CONTENT STANDARDS

The National Research Council in cooperation with a number of other scientific and education associations has established a set of national science content standards for all grade levels, K–12, in an effort to improve the quality of school science. The standards are divided into three categories based upon grade level: K–4, 5–8, and 9–12.

The table on page 161 presents the science content standards for grades K–4, the standards category that applies to the activities contained in this guide. How the activities relate to those standards is then shown in a correlation matrix on pages 162–163. Bulleted standards are those to which a given activity relates to one degree or another and/or for which the activity can serve as a basis for making such associations. Within that matrix, activities are listed by activity number and title, and the content standards are identified by letter and number. For more information concerning the national standards, see *National Science Education Standards* (1996), published by the National Research Council through the National Academy Press in Washington, D.C.

U. UNIFYING CONCEPTS AND PROCESSES	A. SCIENCE AS INQUIRY	B. PHYSICAL SCIENCE	C. LIFE SCIENCE
U-1. Systems, order, and organization U-2. Evidence, models, and explanation U-3. Change, constancy, and measurement U-4. Evolution and equilibrium U-5. Form and function	A-1. Abilities necessary to do scientific inquiry A-2. Understandings about scientific inquiry	B-1. Properties of objects and materials B-2. Position and motion of objects B-3. Light, heat, electricity, and magnetism	C-1. Characteristics of organisms C-2. Life cycles of organisms C-3. Organisms and environments

D. EARTH AND SPACE SCIENCE	E. SCIENCE AND TECHNOLOGY	F. SCIENCE IN PERSONAL AND SOCIAL PERSPECTIVES	G. HISTORY AND NATURE OF SCIENCE
D-1. Properties of earth materials D-2. Objects in the sky D-3. Changes in earth and sky	E-1. Abilities of technological design E-2. Understandings about science and technology E-3. Ability to distinguish between natural objects and objects made by humans	F-1. Personal health F-2. Characteristics and changes in populations F-3. Types of resources F-4. Changes in environments F-5. Science and technology in local challenges	G-1. Science as a human endeavor

Note: Science-Standards categories B (Physical Science) and C (Life Science) are not applicable to this guide and are thus not included in the table below.

Activity Title	National Science Content Standards for Grades K–4																		
	U-1	U-2	U-3	U-4	U-5	A-1	A-2	D-1	D-2	D-3	E-1	E-2	E-3	F-1	F-2	F-3	F-4	F-5	G-1
1. Balloon Kebab		•	•	•		•		•				•							
2. Silver Spiral	•	•	•	•		•	•	•		•		•							•
3. Full of Hot Air	•	•	•	•	•	•	•	•		•	•	•	•						•
4. Unworkable Straw	•	•	•	•	•	•	•	•		•	•	•					•		•
5. Bag Pull		•	•	•	•	•	•	•		•	•	•							•
6. Marshmallow Mash		•	•			•	•	•		•	•	•	•						
7. I'm Under a Lot of Pressure		•	•	•		•	•	•		•		•					•		•
8. Record a Temp		•	•		•	•	•			•		•	•			•			
9. Time Is Energy		•	•			•	•	•		•		•					•		•
10. How Hot Is It?		•	•			•	•	•		•	•	•	•			•			•
11. Free As the Wind	•	•	•		•	•	•	•		•	•	•	•			•	•	•	•
12. To Evap or Not to Evap		•	•			•	•	•		•		•							•
13. Disappearing Water		•	•			•	•	•		•		•							•
14. Rainbow Brite		•	•		•	•	•		•	•		•	•			•			•
15. On Cloud Nine		•	•			•	•		•	•		•	•			•			•
16. Rainy Gauge		•	•		•	•	•			•	•	•	•				•		•
17. Ahoy, Matey	•	•	•		•	•	•			•		•	•				•		•
18. 'Round and 'Round She Goes	•	•	•	•	•	•	•	•		•	•	•							•
19. Are You Dense?	•	•	•		•	•	•	•		•		•	•						•
20. Shooting Waters		•	•	•	•	•	•	•		•		•				•		•	•
21. A Squirty Contest		•	•	•	•	•	•	•		•		•				•		•	•
22. Waves in a Bottle		•	•		•	•	•	•		•	•	•	•						•

Activity Title	National Science Content Standards for Grades K–4																		
	U-1	U-2	U-3	U-4	U-5	A-1	A-2	D-1	D-2	D-3	E-1	E-2	E-3	F-1	F-2	F-3	F-4	F-5	G-1
23. Good-bye Rock—Shake, Rattle, and Roll		•	•			•	•	•		•		•	•				•	•	•
24. Groovy Glacier		•	•		•	•	•	•		•		•	•						•
25. Plant Power		•	•	•	•	•	•	•		•		•	•				•		•
26. Ice Is Nice Unless You're a Rock		•	•			•	•	•		•		•					•		•
27. Rock Fizz		•	•	•		•	•	•		•		•	•				•	•	•
28. Blowing in the Wind	•	•	•	•		•	•	•		•		•	•			•	•	•	•
29. Slowing It Down		•	•			•	•	•		•		•	•			•	•		•
30. Settle Down!		•	•		•	•	•	•		•		•	•				•		•
31. Rock Critter	•	•			•	•	•	•				•	•						•
32. All Rocks Are Not Created Equal	•	•				•	•	•				•	•			•			•
33. Instant Rocks		•	•	•	•	•	•	•		•		•	•			•			•
34. Man Oh Man, Dig Them Bones!	•	•	•	•	•	•		•		•		•	•				•		
35. My Dinosaur Name Is . . .	•	•	•	•	•	•		•		•		•	•				•		
36. Dinosaur Diorama		•				•		•				•	•						
37. Mystery Footprints	•	•	•	•		•	•	•		•		•	•						•
38. A Mite Tite Is Alrite	•	•	•	•	•	•	•	•		•	•	•	•				•		•
39. Sinking		•	•	•	•	•	•	•		•		•	•	•			•	•	•
40. Moon Man	•	•	•		•	•	•		•	•	•	•	•						•
41. Star Pictures	•	•	•		•	•	•		•		•	•				•			•
42. Stargazer	•	•	•		•	•	•		•			•	•			•			•